"How fabulous is this! A brief primer on DBT written by one of the world's experts in DBT treatment and research. Even better: Practical exercises are included throughout. My advice to you is to try this out. You won't regret it." **—Marsha M. Linehan, PhD, ABPP**, Professor and Director, Behavioral Research and Training Clinics, Department of Psychology at the University of Washington

Dialectical Behavior Therapy
for Emotion Dysregulation

A NORTON PROFESSIONAL BOOK

Dialectical Behavior Therapy for Emotion Dysregulation

Shelley McMain

Carmen Wiebe

SERIES EDITORS: Paula Ravitz and Robert Maunder

W. W. NORTON & COMPANY

New York | London

For information about permission to reproduce selections from this book, write to
Permissions, W. W. Norton & Company, Inc., 500 Fifth Avenue, New York, NY 10110

For information about special discounts for bulk purchases, please contact W. W. Norton
Special Sales at specialsales@wwnorton.com or 800-233-4830

Manufacturing by Quad Graphics
Book design by Kristina Kachele Design, llc
Production manager: Leeann Graham

Library of Congress Cataloging-in-Publication Data
Wiebe, Carmen.
Dialectical behavior therapy for emotion dysregulation / Carmen Wiebe, Shelley McMain. — First edition.
pages cm. — (Psychotherapy essentials to go)
"A Norton professional book."
Includes bibliographical references.
ISBN 978-0-393-70825-7 (pbk.)
1. Borderline personality disorder — Treatment — Handbooks, manuals, etc. 2. Emotional problems —
Treatment — Handbooks, manuals, etc. 3. Emotions — Handbooks, manuals, etc. 4. Dialectical behavior
therapy — Handbooks, manuals, etc. I. McMain, Shelley. II. Title.
RC569.5.B67W54 2013
616.85'85206—dc23
                2013008228

ISBN: 978-0-393-70825-7 (pbk.)

W. W. Norton & Company, Inc., 500 Fifth Avenue, New York, N.Y. 10110
www.wwnorton.com
W. W. Norton & Company Ltd., Castle House, 75/76 Wells Street, London W1T 3QT

1 2 3 4 5 6 7 8 9 0

To Marsha Linehan, the developer of Dialectical Behavior Therapy, without whose work this book would not have been possible.

Shelley McMain, PhD, a researcher, clinician, and educator, is head of the Borderline Personality Disorder (BPD) Clinic as well as head of Personality Disorder Capacity Building and Research in the Women's Program at the Centre for Addiction and Mental Health. She is also Associate Professor in the Department of Psychiatry at the University of Toronto.

Carmen Wiebe, MD, is Assistant Professor in the Department of Psychiatry at the University of Toronto, where she coordinates Dialectical Behavior Therapy education for the postgraduate program. She also works in the Borderline Personality Disorder Clinic at the Centre for Addiction and Mental Health.

Paula Ravitz, MD, is Associate Professor, Morgan Firestone Psychotherapy Chair, and Associate Director of the Psychotherapy, Health Humanities, and Education Scholarship Division for the Department of Psychiatry at the University of Toronto, where she leads IPT training. She is also the director of the Mt. Sinai Psychotherapy Institute. Her clinical practice, teaching, and research focus on IPT and attachment-informed psychotherapy.

Robert Maunder, MD, is Associate Professor in the Department of Psychiatry at the University of Toronto and head of research for Mount Sinai Hospital's Department of Psychiatry. His primary research interest is the role of interpersonal attachment on health.

Contents

Acknowledgments

Producing *Psychotherapy Essentials to Go* has depended on and benefited from the support and expertise of many people. We wish to acknowledge and thank Marsha Linehan, the developer of Dialectical Behavior Therapy, who, with others, has built the foundation from which this treatment has grown. We are grateful to the contributing authors whose hard work, wisdom, and creativity as educators and clinicians are represented; the Ontario Ministry of Health and Long Term Care who provided funding to the educational outreach pilot project team of the Northern Psychiatric Outreach Program at the Centre for Addiction and Mental Health (CAMH); Nancy McNaughton and the University of Toronto Standardized Patient Program; Robert Swenson and the Ontario Psychiatric Outreach Program; the University of Toronto Department of Psychiatry; the Mount Sinai Hospital Department of Psychiatry; Molyn

Leszcz and the Morgan Firestone Psychotherapy Chair; Scott Mitchell; the executive directors and healthcare workers at the Canadian Mental Health Association's northern Ontario branch; and Andrea Costella Dawson and Sophie Hagen of W. W. Norton. We also wish to thank Robert Cooke at the CAMH, as well as Tom and Reet Mae and Ryan Hannabee of Mae Studios, Bhadra Lokuge, Connie Kim, Lynn Fisher, Risa Bramon-Garcia, Charlie Swenson, Janice Kuo, and the actors who brought the material to life.

Series Introduction

Psychotherapy works. Meta-analyses demonstrate that psychotherapy reduces the symptoms and impact of the mental disorders that most commonly interfere with people's lives, including depression, anxiety, and the extraordinary challenges that emerge from concurrent addictions, mental illnesses, and personality disorders. The consensus treatment guidelines that provide clinicians with evidence-based direction for treating depression, anxiety, and other mental disorders recommend psychotherapy, sometimes as a first line of treatment.

At the same time, practicing *effective* psychotherapy is very challenging. For one thing, treatment guidelines recommend specific modalities of psychotherapy for specific disorders, such as Interpersonal Psychotherapy (IPT) for depression, Cognitive Behavioral Therapy (CBT) for depression or anxiety, Motivational Interviewing (MI) for mental health issues and substance abuse disorders, and Dialectical Behavior Therapy (DBT) for borderline personality disorder. Therapists working at the front lines of mental healthcare see *all* of these problems, but acquiring extensive supervision, training, and certification in any one of these modalities is costly and challenging, and being an expert in all types of psychotherapy is virtually impossible. How can a front-line therapist use the core skills of different modalities of psychotherapy effectively to help his or her clients overcome the debilitating effects of mental illness?

Psychotherapy Essentials to Go responds to the challenge that therapists who are not (yet) experts face in acquiring the core skills of psychotherapy. It is designed to be useful for both new therapists and those who are more experienced but want to learn the core techniques of different types of psychotherapy. It also is a refresher course on the techniques that experienced therapists are already familiar with.

This project emerged in response to the needs of mental healthcare workers who were facing extraordinary challenges. Working in community clinics in remote, underserviced areas, these clinicians were unable to provide psychotherapy to their clients because they had minimal psychotherapy training and limited means of acquiring it. Caseloads were often heavy and resources for referring clients to psychotherapists were extremely limited. These clinicians wanted but were unable to use psychotherapeutic techniques to help their clients suffering from depression, anxiety, and concurrent disorders. Needless to say, it was not feasible for these health workers to obtain the training, observation, and close supervision that are required to become experts in specific modalities of psychotherapy. Surely, there was a better alternative than providing no psychotherapy at all!

Drawing on the wealth of expertise of the contributing authors in this series, who are all faculty or staff at teaching hospitals affiliated with the University of Toronto, we created the videos that are at the core of the *Psychotherapy Essentials to Go* materials, as well as all of the accompanying lesson plans in order to meet the needs of clinicians and their clients. The materials worked. We tested the materials that we developed with healthcare workers of several disciplines and levels of experience including the caseworkers in community mental healthcare clinics whose needs initiated the project, medical students, nurses, family medicine and psychiatry residents, and social workers. Their knowledge increased, they used the techniques they had learned, and they reported that they had become more confident and effective clinicians, even with difficult clients. Even seasoned therapists benefited from brushing up on the specific therapy protocols (Ravitz et al., 2013).

The first five books and DVDs of the *Psychotherapy Essentials to Go* series teach the skills of Motivational Interviewing, Cognitive Behavioral Therapy (for anxiety and for depression), Dialectical Behavior Therapy, and Interpersonal Psychotherapy. These materials are not intended to replace full training in these evidence-supported psychotherapies; rather, they introduce and demonstrate techniques that clinicians and students can integrate into their care of people with common mental health problems.

The sixth book and its accompanying DVD address psychotherapy effectiveness across every modality of therapy. Regardless of which type of psychotherapy a therapist provides, doing psychotherapy requires therapists to be flexible and responsive to their clients. Also therapists and clients must form and sustain a strong working relationship: the therapeutic alliance. In every modality of psychotherapy, a good therapeutic alliance leads to better clinical outcomes. With some clients the challenges encountered in forming and maintaining an alliance provide a window into the interpersonal difficulties that the clients experience in their other important relationships. This final book on psychotherapy effectiveness synthesizes the most important common factors of psychotherapies and provides a therapist with an approach to understanding and managing challenges to establishing and maintaining a therapeutic alliance.

Learning psychotherapy means *changing how you behave* as a clinician—and changing habitual behavior is notoriously difficult. Learning new professional behavior takes time and practice—you need to *experience* a new way of behaving. It isn't enough to read about it or hear about it. Experiential learning is most effective when it includes demonstration, modeling, and practice. For each book in the series, we suggest that you first watch the DVD, then read the accompanying text, and then follow the instructions in the lesson plans to practice and consolidate your learning. Take the quiz before starting this process in order to assess your baseline knowledge, and then take it again after having completed all four of the lessons, in order to assess your progress. Afterward, use the summary card of practice reminders in your daily clinical work.

For those interested in more training, further reading and clinical supervision are recommended. We hope that the techniques presented in these introductory *Psychotherapy Essentials to Go* materials will expand your clinical repertoire and will improve your competence and confidence in working with clients with mental health problems.

A couple of notes about language. First, those who provide care and treatment for people with mental health problems, and individuals who receive that care, prefer a wide range of names for those roles, and some have strong feelings about their preferences. For the sake of consistency, throughout this series we refer to the former individuals as "therapists" (occasionally opting for "clinicians" for the sake of some variety of expression) and the latter as "clients." We do this in spite of the fact that some modalities of psychotherapy are explicit about which terms are preferable (for example, IPT manuals refer to the person receiving the therapy as a patient, in keeping with the centrality of the medical model in IPT). We hope these are read to be the inclusive and nonprescriptive choices that are intended. Second, although pronouns in English are gendered, the gender of the therapists and clients we are discussing is usually irrelevant. We have opted for the phrases "he or she" and "his or her" except for a few passages where pronouns were required so frequently that it became too awkward. In those sections we have settled on one gender indiscriminately, with the intention that the "hes" and "shes" will balance out in the end.

Paula Ravitz and Bob Maunder

1 :: Introduction to Dialectical Behavior Therapy for Emotion Dysregulation

Dialectical Behavior Therapy (DBT) was originally developed by Dr. Marsha Linehan to treat chronically suicidal women with Borderline Personality Disorder (Linehan, 1993a, 1993b). Several research studies have demonstrated that DBT reduces suicide attempts and nonsuicidal self-injurious behaviors, emergency department visits, hospital admission rates and lengths, and levels of depression and anger. To date, DBT in its original and adapted forms is the psychotherapy with the strongest evidence base for this population (Bohus et al., 2004; Carter et al., 2010; Clarkin, Levy, Lenzenweger, & Kernberg, 2007; Koons et al., 2001; Linehan, Armstrong, Suarez, Allmon, & Heard, 1991; Linehan et al., 1999, 2002, 2006; McMain et al., 2009; McMain, Guimond, Streiner, Cardish, & Links, 2012; Verheul et al., 2003).

Most studies of DBT have focused on women, because in clinical settings Borderline Personality Disorder is more commonly diagnosed in women than in men. However, there is preliminary evidence that supports the use of DBT for men with similar problems. DBT has been adapted (Dimeff & Koerner, 2007) for a wide range of difficult-to-treat populations, such as for people with eating disorders, people with substance use disorders, people in correctional settings, suicidal adolescents (Miller, Rathus, & Linehan, 2007), people with treatment-resistant depression, and people with intellectual disabilities.

Overall, DBT and its adaptations are designed for people with complex, severe problems who engage in impulsive and self-damaging behaviors in response to overwhelming emotional dysregulation. DBT targets the combination of emotional dysregulation and impulsive behavior, which is a hallmark of Borderline Personality Disorder but also occurs in other circumstances, particularly when several challenging disorders co-occur. Problems that are associated with emotional dysregulation and behavioral impulsivity can be addressed independently of diagnostic labels; therefore, in practice it is probably not essential to have a particular diagnosis in order to offer DBT or to integrate DBT techniques into other approaches.

In this introductory section, we provide a brief overview of DBT and then discuss some concepts and techniques from it that may be integrated into general psychotherapeutic treatment when it is not possible to provide the full model. Research is currently under way to examine whether specific elements of DBT are effective in the absence of the full treatment package. To date, there are preliminary data supporting the use of DBT skills training on its own (Soler et al., 2009), as well as selected DBT-informed principles or strategies (Turner, 2000).

STRUCTURE AND THEORETICAL FOUNDATION
Treatment Modes and Their Functions

In its standard outpatient format for the treatment of Borderline Personality Disorder, DBT consists of four concurrent modes of treatment delivery: weekly individual therapy, weekly group skills training, between-session phone coaching, and weekly therapist-consultation team meetings. In standard DBT programs, clients receive these four components in an outpatient setting over the course of 1 year.

Successful treatment for complex, multidisordered individuals with emotional dysregulation must fulfill five functions: learning new skills, generalizing new behaviors, improving motivation to change, ensuring the individual's environment supports change, and supporting therapists. Each of the four DBT treatment modes addresses one of these functions. In addition, various family or social network-oriented interventions may be used to assist individuals in shaping their environments to reinforce desired changes and avoid reinforcing problematic behaviors (see Table 1).

Table 1. Functions and Modes of Dialectical Behavior Therapy

Function	Mode	Details
Learning Healthy Coping Skills	SKILLS TRAINING	2 to 2.5 hours per week of psychoeducational group therapy
Generalizing New Behaviors	TELEPHONE CONSULTATION	24-hour availability for skills coaching in daily life, including crisis management
Improving Motivation to Change	INDIVIDUAL THERAPY	1 to 1.5 hours per week Apply skills to the client's personal life Analyze the factors that interfere with substituting effective behaviors for dysfunctional ones
Structuring the Environment to Support Change	No specific mode	This function can be addressed in many ways, such as teaching skills to family members, offering couple or family counseling, or having meetings with the client's personal or professional support network The therapist's environment (colleagues and management) also needs to support the therapist in providing compassionate and evidence-based care
Supporting Therapists	CONSULTATION TEAM	1 to 2 hours per week Mutual support, validation, encouragement, and help with problem solving Maintain consistency with DBT principles

Adapting DBT for inpatient, residential, or day treatment settings requires finding creative ways to ensure that these functions are fulfilled (for information on DBT adaptations, see Dimeff & Koerner, 2007). In fact, anyone wishing to provide effective assistance to a person with severe emotional dysregulation should keep all five functions in mind and devise a treatment plan that addresses them as well as possible. Some settings may not be able to provide a skills group, for example, but an individual therapist may be able to incorporate teaching skills into individual treatment sessions. If couples counseling is not available, an individual therapist may be able to work on interpersonal skills to improve relationships within a client's social network. If 24-hour phone coaching is not available, perhaps coaching calls could be taken during more limited hours, or the therapist could help the client teach a friend or family member how to offer effective skills reminders during a crisis.

Theoretical Basis of DBT
DBT evolved out of Linehan's efforts to apply Cognitive Behavioral Therapy to women who have histories of chronic self-harm and suicidality. Cognitive Behavioral Therapy is informed by Learning Theory, from which one can extract three fundamental principles:

- learning may be conditioned by association (classical conditioning),
- learning may be reinforced by consequences (operant conditioning), and
- learning may occur through observing others (modeling).

Linehan discovered that Cognitive Behavioral Therapy's focus on change, including efforts to correct thinking errors, was experienced by clients as invalidating, which led to an increase in anger and therapy dropouts. She felt that the emphasis on change needed to be balanced by an emphasis on acceptance. To find this balance, she incorporated features of Rogerian client-centered therapy, Western contemplative practices, and especially Zen mindfulness into the treatment.

Next, in order to integrate these two opposites—change and acceptance—Linehan borrowed from dialectical philosophy, which describes the process of combining elements from opposing poles in order to form a creative synthesis.

Thus, the three theories that inform DBT are the following:

- Learning Theory, with its emphasis on identifying all the variables that promote or hinder change;
- Zen philosophy, with its emphasis on accepting each moment as it is; and
- Dialectical philosophy, which emphasizes that reality is composed of apparent opposites and which proposes searching for ways that two opposing ideas can both be true.

DIALECTICAL BEHAVIOR THERAPY: SELECTED TECHNIQUES

In the accompanying DVD and learning guide, we describe two techniques to help therapists maintain compassion for clients with severe emotional dysregulation, as well as four sets of strategies that may be used in individual sessions with clients. For a complete description of all therapist strategies in DBT, therapists should refer to the treatment manuals *Cognitive-Behavioral Treatment of Borderline Personality Disorder* (1993a) and *Skills Training Manual for Treating Borderline Personality Disorder* (1993b) by Marsha Linehan.

The Biosocial Theory and Assumptions About Clients

Zen philosophy emphasizes the value of a nonjudgmental and compassionate attitude. It is essential that clients learn to be nonjudgmental and compassionate toward themselves, and that therapists adopt similar attitudes toward their clients. Compassion may be defined as being empathic toward another's suffering and wanting to help. A compassionate approach does not have to be unfailingly soothing and supportive: at times, an empathically derived wish to help can require confrontation. Nonetheless, negative emotions such as frustration or anger must be expressed in a way that is genuine yet avoids being hostile or rejecting.

One essential tool that DBT therapists use to maintain patience and understanding for their clients is the biosocial theory, which views an emotionally dysregulated client's current problems as the inevitable result of the interaction between his or her temperament and an invalidating environment. Therapists can use the biosocial theory to avoid blaming or rejecting statements such as "she's just doing this for attention," "she should know better," or "she's trying to manipulate me." The biosocial theory informs the case formulation, which helps the therapist keep the treatment focused, and it also helps the client view her own difficulties in a self-validating and hopeful light.

Another tool that therapists use to stay energized and nonjudgmental is the set of DBT assumptions about clients, which are listed in the learning guide. These assumptions are helpful beliefs that allow therapists to maintain a positive and open approach with their challenging clients.

Selected Sets of DBT Therapist Strategies

DBT therapists draw from 12 sets of treatment strategies. Any of these strategies can be integrated into other treatments outside of a standard DBT program. We have chosen four specific techniques to highlight here—validation, commitment strategies, behavioral chain analysis, and skills training—which we believe are transferable to any setting and which can be particularly useful in addressing the problems that arise during work with individuals who suffer from severe emotional dysregulation.

VALIDATION

Validation entails communicating an understanding of the client's experience and conveying what makes sense about it. It is a fundamental strategy for working effectively with emotionally sensitive people. On its own, validation is not enough to achieve change, but without it there can be no change. Validation is essential to building trust and a strong therapeutic alliance.

Therapists working with individuals who have severe emotional dysregulation need to weave validating statements throughout every interaction, and especially before offering help with problem solving. Even when clients ask directly for help, a therapist's response that does not include validation is likely to be experienced as aversive and unsupportive. Whenever the therapist thinks that the client is disengaged or not fully on board with a plan, the first strategy to try is validation: convey that there is something that makes sense about the client's thoughts, emotions, or actions. Once the client feels understood, it will be easier to resume problem solving (Linehan, 1997).

COMMITMENT STRATEGIES

Strategies to build commitment are also required to set the stage for effective problem solving. A prerequisite for problem solving is that the client has identified a desire to get help with a specific problem. Even when clients ask directly for help, it is important to ensure that they are committed to finding ways to solve the problem and that they agree with the potential utility of spending some of this session talking about it with a therapist. Commitment strategies can be used to ensure that there is a commitment, to build and strengthen commitments, and to troubleshoot any foreseeable obstacles to following through on a commitment.

BEHAVIORAL CHAIN ANALYSIS

Behavioral chain analysis is the fundamental problem-solving technique of DBT. It is a systematic method of breaking down all the elements leading up to and occurring immediately after a behavior in order to figure out what contributed to the behavior. The "behavioral chain analysis" is the first level and involves examining one instance of a behavior. The next level, "behavioral analysis," involves developing an understanding of the factors that are controlling specific classes of behaviors or similar types of behaviors. Behavioral chain analyses can be used to analyze functional or dysfunctional behaviors. The analysis allows problematic elements in the chain of events to be identified and then changed. Throughout the analysis, both the client and therapist need to brainstorm solutions to each problematic element; solutions may include skills, emotional exposure, cognitive restructuring, or changing contingencies. Productive behaviors are also highlighted and reinforced so that the client will continue to use them in the future. A behavioral chain analysis has five steps:

1. *Identify the specific behavior*: The first step in the chain analysis is to be clear about which behavior is being analyzed. A chain analysis does not examine a "typical" instance of a behavior but focuses on one specific occurrence. Important details about the behavior include the day on which it occurred, the time, the location, how long it lasted, and how severe it was. Relevant behaviors may be overt actions such as self-harm, an anger outburst, a binge-eating episode, or an incident of substance use. They can also be covert experiences such as intense painful emotions, dysfunctional thoughts, or urges to engage in harmful actions.

2. *Identify vulnerabilities*: Many factors are likely to influence why the client's behavior occurred on a particular day. Some may be related to the distant past, such as a history of childhood abuse, but some may be in the recent past, such as an interpersonal conflict, a medication change, or a physical illness.

3. *Identify the prompting event*: It is important to search for a specific event that precipitated the behavior. Often there is an interpersonal event that can be seen as the first link in the chain toward the behavior, although triggers can also be internal, such as a flashback or a physical sensation. The prompting event can sometimes be elicited by inquiring about what was going on when the client first noticed an urge to engage in the problem behavior.

4. *Identify the links that connect the prompting event to the behavior*: All emotions, thoughts, urges, and actions that occurred between the prompting event and the behavior are of interest. Productive or healthy responses need to be strengthened, and problematic ones need to be altered. In particular, careful examination of the client's

decision-making process is crucial. It is useful to try to isolate the moment when the client made the decision to engage in the behavior (e.g., he or she may have had the thought "I refuse to tolerate this pain any longer"), because this allows him or her to develop greater understanding and control over impulsive behaviors that can seem to happen instantly or out of the blue.

5. *Identify the consequences*: Events that occur immediately after the problem behavior may serve to reinforce it, such as emotional relief after self-harm. Inadvertent reinforcers may include increased attention (positive or negative) from important people in the client's life, such as the whole family meeting him or her in the emergency department—even if the family members are angry.

Clients may find that engaging in a behavioral chain analysis is difficult, but it is crucial that the therapist does not avoid this technique as a result. A fruitful, collaborative chain analysis is interwoven with a generous use of validation; otherwise, clients can become overwhelmed. It may also be necessary to review the client's commitment both to meeting his or her goals and to engaging in problem solving in order to meet these goals.

TEACHING SKILLS

One of the ways that clients can alter the problematic elements identified through behavioral chain analyses is to learn and apply new coping skills. In a standard DBT program, coping skills are taught formally in a group setting. A 6-month curriculum—which is covered twice in a standard DBT program—can be found in the *Skills Training Manual for Treating*

Borderline Personality Disorder (1993b) by Marsha Linehan. If a group is not available, these skills can also be taught individually, either as they seem relevant, or more rigorously (e.g., devoting part of each individual session to skills teaching and review).

There are four modules of skills in DBT. *Mindfulness* skills help clients increase their awareness and acceptance of themselves and their environment. *Distress Tolerance* skills provide alternatives to acting on impulsive urges. *Emotion Regulation* skills teach clients how to understand and change emotions. *Interpersonal Effectiveness* skills focus on clear, direct, and assertive communication. The DVD demonstrates how to integrate Distress Tolerance skills teaching into a session focused on helping a client eliminate self-harm.

TRAINING

This DVD and learning guide are not intended to enable therapists to develop adherence or competence in DBT. A plethora of DBT training opportunities exist. These include formal workshops, in-person or online courses, Internet sites, videotapes and DVDs, and books. A gold standard initial course in DBT is the 10-day intensive training from Behavioral Tech, LLC. This consists of two 5-day workshops that must be attended by a minimum of four members from the same team who are working toward establishing a standard DBT program. As with any other psychotherapy, expertise in DBT is developed through a combination of formal learning, close study of the treatment manuals, and supervision while practicing the treatment.

2 :: Learning Objectives

The following objectives will help you to focus your learning as you read the learning guide, review the DVD, and do the reflective exercises.

At the end of this book, we hope that you will be able to achieve these goals:

1. Understand the development of emotional dysregulation and explain this to clients.
2. Communicate your understanding of what makes sense about a client's experience (i.e., validation).
3. Use commitment strategies to increase your clients' motivation to work on problems and increase the likelihood that they will follow through on commitments.

4. Use problem-solving strategies to help clients reduce or eliminate impulsive behaviors, including self-harm.

5. Coach clients to use distress tolerance skills during extreme emotion dysregulation and crises.

Shelley McMain and Carmen Wiebe

3 :: Fundamentals of Dialectical Behavior Therapy

THEORETICAL BASIS OF DIALECTICAL BEHAVIOR THERAPY

Dialectical Behavior Therapy is a cognitive behavioral treatment that was developed by Marsha Linehan, who is a psychologist and scientist working at the University of Washington. DBT is grounded in three theories: Learning Theory, Zen philosophy, and dialectical philosophy.

The first pillar of DBT is Learning Theory, which states that behavioral patterns become established through association with specific antecedents, through reinforcement by specific consequences, and by observing other people's behaviors. Behavioral patterns can thus be modified by changing the antecedents and the consequences and by modeling different behaviors.

The second pillar of DBT is Zen philosophy. From this perspective, suffering results from becoming attached to things being a particular way. From the perspective of Zen, the key to reducing suffering is to accept reality as it is. DBT's emphasis on validation and acceptance flows directly from Zen philosophy.

ZEN PHILOSOPHY

Suffering stems from becoming attached to things being a particular way.

The key to reducing suffering is to **accept** reality as it is.

Third, dialectical philosophy is an overarching framework for the entire program of treatment in DBT. In essence, DBT involves finding a balance between two opposites: a focus on change on the one hand and a focus on acceptance on the other. Dialectical philosophy proposes that elements from opposing poles can be combined in a creative synthesis.

DIALECTICAL PHILOSOPHY

Finding a balance between two opposites:
a focus on **change**
and a focus on **acceptance**.

DIALECTICAL PHILOSOPHY

In any given interaction, a therapist moves between pushing hard for change and, at the same time, communicating to the client that everything is perfect as it is. The tension between these two opposites can be resolved in a creative synthesis that emphasizes how both sides can be true.

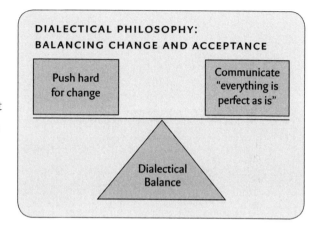

DIALECTICAL PHILOSOPHY: BALANCING CHANGE AND ACCEPTANCE

Push hard for change

Communicate "everything is perfect as is"

Dialectical Balance

DBT was developed originally for people with chronic suicidal behavior. However, it was later adapted to a range of different client populations. The common denominator that cuts across these adaptations is that the individuals have severe problems regulating their moods and also regulating their behaviors. Although there is some evidence supporting the effectiveness of DBT for populations with problems other than BPD, more research is required to assess these adaptations.

WHO IS SUITABLE FOR DBT?

- DBT is an evidence-based program that was originally developed for people with chronic suicidal behavior.

- Adaptations may be helpful for a range of clients who have severe emotional and behavioral dysregulation.

STAYING COMPASSIONATE

Clients with severe emotional dysregulation often challenge a therapist's ability to be compassionate, no matter how experienced the therapist is. Before we discuss the strategies that are used in sessions with clients, it is useful to introduce a set of principles that therapists can use to stay grounded and compassionate with challenging client populations.

The first principle is that having a theoretical understanding of how people develop emotional dysregulation can help a therapist to stay grounded. The biosocial theory is "the story" that reminds us why it makes perfect sense that this person is behaving the way he is. Giving ourselves an explanation of dysregulated behavior allows us to remain patient and nonjudgmental in situations where we might otherwise feel frustrated or rejecting.

Emotion dysregulation is viewed as stemming from two primary sources: the biological, and the social or environmental (Linehan, 1993a; Crowell, Beauchaine, & Linehan, 2009).

On the biological side, someone who develops emotion dysregulation may be likely to have been born with the inherited trait of impulsivity and to have a biological tendency toward an emotionally sensitive temperament.

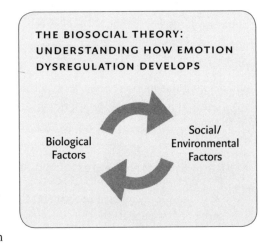

THE BIOSOCIAL THEORY: UNDERSTANDING HOW EMOTION DYSREGULATION DEVELOPS

Biological Factors

Social/ Environmental Factors

An emotionally sensitive temperament refers to three things:

- a tendency to be very quick to react to emotional stimuli;
- a tendency to have very intense emotional reactions; and
- a tendency to take longer than average after an emotional reaction to return to an emotional baseline.

THE BIOSOCIAL THEORY:
UNDERSTANDING EMOTION DYSREGULATION

BIOLOGICAL FACTORS
Trait Impulsivity

Emotionally Sensitive
Temperament

- High sensitivity
- High intensity
- Slower than average
  return to baseline

SOCIAL FACTORS
Invalidating Environment

Examples include:

- Trauma, abuse, neglect
- Lack of emotional attunement
- Ignoring, criticizing, or
  dismissing expression of
  emotion
- Reinforcing out-of-control
  emotional displays

Although impulsivity and emotional sensitivity on their own are risk factors for psychological problems, they do not necessarily lead to problems. With the right kind of care-giving environment, such individuals can turn out to be well adjusted. It is the interaction between these traits and a particular type of environment that leads to the development of emotional dysregulation.

We use the term "invalidating environment" to refer not only to extreme experiences like abuse and neglect but also to subtler ways in which a parent may not be attuned to a child's needs, such as ignoring, criticizing, or dismissing emotional expression, or giving in repeatedly to temper tantrums and thus reinforcing out-of-control emotional displays.

The two arrows in the diagram indicate that it is not just the presence of biological and social factors that lead to emotion dysregulation; it's how they affect each other. A sensitive, intense individual is likely to elicit more invalidating responses from the environment. In turn, the invalidating response makes a sensitive individual more upset and

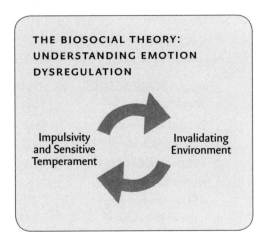

THE BIOSOCIAL THEORY: UNDERSTANDING EMOTION DYSREGULATION

Impulsivity and Sensitive Temperament

Invalidating Environment

more reactive. Her emotional reactions put further stress on her caregivers, which leads to more invalidation, and so on. At the same time, a highly invalidating environment can contribute to increased sensitivity in an individual who is otherwise not predisposed to an emotionally sensitive temperament. It is the *transaction* between the environment and the individual that results in emotion dysregulation problems.

When this pattern becomes ingrained over years, an individual can end up feeling utterly out of control of her emotions. In her experience, there is no solution to the cycle other than using impulsive, self-destructive means to become numb from her intense pain.

Another way to stay compassionate is to adopt a set of assumptions about clients. These are not empirically validated facts; they are helpful beliefs that allow us to let go of judgmental or blaming thoughts about our clients.

STAYING COMPASSIONATE: EIGHT DBT ASSUMPTIONS

1. "Patients are doing the best they can" (Linehan, 1993a, p. 106).
2. "Patients want to improve" (Linehan, 1993a, p. 106).
3. "Patients need to do better, try harder, and be more motivated to change" (Linehan, 1993a, p. 106).
4. "Patients may not have caused all of their own problems, but they have to solve them anyway" (Linehan, 1993a, p. 107).
5. The lives of suicidal or emotionally dysregulated individuals are unbearable as they are currently being lived (Linehan, 1993a).
6. "Patients must learn new behaviors in all relevant contexts" (Linehan, 1993a, p. 107).
7. It is not a client's fault if he or she does not change (Linehan, 1993a).
8. Therapists working with difficult clients need support (Linehan, 1993a).

4 :: Validation

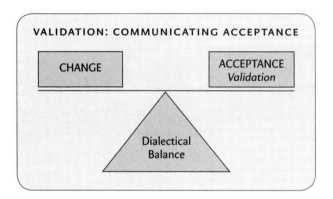

VALIDATION: COMMUNICATING ACCEPTANCE

| CHANGE | | ACCEPTANCE *Validation* |

Dialectical Balance

Validation is one of the core strategies in DBT. Validation balances out the focus on change. Marsha Linehan integrated a strong focus on acceptance and validation in this treatment model because she discovered that clients often find it highly aversive if therapists focus too much on strategies for change.

A therapist validates a client by stating what makes sense or what is reasonable about a client's behavior within a specific context. **In DBT every change strategy is surrounded by validation.**

VALIDATION

Communicate what is understandable or reasonable about a client's behavior.

WHY VALIDATE?

Validation:

- Soothes clients and decreases emotional arousal
- Helps the clients understand that many aspects of their experiences are normal
- Teaches the clients to self-validate and trust themselves
- Strengthens the alliance between the therapist and each client

There are several reasons why it is important to validate. First, conveying an accurate understanding of your client is generally experienced as soothing, and thereby it really helps to decrease your client's emotional arousal. Also, validation helps the client understand that many aspects of his or her experience are normal, so it helps to teach the client to validate himself or herself and to trust the experience. And it's critical for strengthening your alliance with your client.

VALIDATION

Find the wisdom or grain of truth in the client's behavior.

*Though at times it may be challenging to find, there's always **something** reasonable about your client's response.*

Linehan (1997) discusses six ways to validate clients. In this section, we briefly describe these different ways of conveying validation.

She explains that the first, and perhaps most obvious, way to be validating is to be fully awake and alert to what your client is communi-

cating. Listen to your client without bias and without thinking judgmental thoughts while he or she is talking. Try to really take in what your
client is talking about.

One of the reasons why
appearing interested is so
important is that it communicates to your client the
following thought: "I consider
you important enough to get
my full attention." Bear in

> **VALIDATING**
> **Appear Interested**
>
> Be alert and interested in what your client is saying.
> Practice unbiased, nonjudgmental listening.
> Take your client seriously.

mind that clients whose behaviors are extreme and difficult to understand are often not taken seriously, so your full attention is often a
powerful new experience.

> **VALIDATING**
> **Paraphrase**
>
> Reflect or summarize the client's thoughts, urges, feelings, or emotions.
> Communicate the essence of what the client says, reorganizing the content
>   and restating it in a coherent way.

Another way to validate is to simply reflect back to your client what
it is that he or she is communicating. Paraphrasing offers an unbiased
summary of the client's thoughts, urges, feelings, or emotions.

Paraphrasing communicates the essence of what your client is saying
to you. It does not mean parroting back exactly what the client said; rather it may involve reorganizing the content of what he or she has said in a
clear and coherent way.

VALIDATING
Mind Read

Convey the client's unexpressed emotions, thoughts, or urges.

Reflect your understanding of the client and her or his internal experiences (i.e., suffering and pain, difficulty of making changes).

A third way of validating is to convey what a client leaves unexpressed. Mind reading involves accurately reflecting the emotions, thoughts, or urges that have not been stated directly. By doing this a therapist can bring something the client hasn't shared directly into the conversation.

Mind reading reflects an understanding of the client that goes beyond just what has been stated. Most of us want to have the experience when we're with somebody that he or she can understand us without us having to spell everything out. When this occurs it can be very validating.

We won't always be accurate in our reading of a client's unexpressed experience, so be willing to be corrected.

Naturally, we can't actually read someone's mind, and our attempts to put unarticulated thoughts and feelings into words may not always be accurate. If your client rejects your efforts at mind reading, you've got to be willing to let it go.

The fourth way of validating is to focus on what makes sense in the client's behaviors, urges, thoughts, and feelings, based on her past learning, dysfunctional thinking, or biology.

For example, it could be that your client's self-criticism makes perfect sense because all her life she has been criticized by a parent. Or it might make perfect sense that a client has a hard time getting out of bed in the morning because most people who are depressed have a really hard time getting up in the morning.

> **VALIDATING**
> **Make Sense Based on History**
>
> Communicate how your client's problems, behaviors, urges, thoughts, and feelings make sense based on:
> - Past learning
> - Faulty thinking
> - Biological differences or disorder

> *Not all behavior is valid or reasonable so don't validate behaviors that aren't sensible.*
>
> *Search for and highlight the specific aspect of the behavior that does make sense.*

Take care not to validate behaviors that aren't reasonable. A therapist would not tell a depressed client who missed a morning session because he was too tired that it made sense to miss the session. It doesn't make sense for the client to miss a treatment session if he's depressed and needs treatment.

The idea is not to respond with validation to every behavior but to search for and highlight the aspect of a behavior that is reasonable.

Normalizing validates the client's behavior in terms of what is true for most people. Here, we are searching for the kernel of wisdom in the client's response and conveying why this response makes sense in terms of normal behavior.

> **VALIDATING**
> **Normalize What Is True for Most People**
>
> Normalize and depathologize a client's response.

This could mean, for example, saying to an individual who is really anxious and having difficulty thinking clearly, "It makes perfect sense that you would have a hard time thinking clearly, given how anxious you are. Most of us, when we get anxious, can't think clearly."

The essence is that you are communicating to the individual that his behavior is normal. This is important because many of our clients invalidate their own behaviors and tend to see themselves in pathological terms, even when they are having normal reactions. Finding a way to help them feel normal becomes an important way to help them validate.

Finally, it is validating to be genuine in your relationship with your client. This means treating your client as a capable and competent person rather than responding to her as someone who is fragile. This entails interacting with your clients in a genuine, direct manner. Being radically genuine means talking in the same way that you might talk with your sister or your best friend or your mother or your father. You can say things directly because you are confident that your words are not going to make your client fall apart emotionally.

Another way to be radically genuine at times may involve cheerleading a client who doesn't believe that he is capable. It could mean saying to somebody, "Hey, I totally believe you can do it even though you don't believe you can do it."

VALIDATING
Be Radically Genuine

Treat the client as a capable, effective, and reasonable individual rather than someone who is fragile.
Interact in a genuine, direct, "ordinary" manner.
"Cheerlead"—be hopeful and encouraging.

This manner of communication is powerful and validating because it conveys your confidence in your client's capabilities.

To summarize, here are Linehan's (1997) six ways to validate clients:

1. **Fully attend.** Listen to your client with full attention, without bias or judgment, to really take in what she or he is talking about.
2. **Paraphrase.** Reflect back the essence of what your client is saying to you.
3. **Mind read.** Try to communicate what is not expressed directly—unarticulated thoughts, feelings, and urges.
4. **Make sense.** Explain the reasons behind your client's behaviors, urges, thoughts, and feelings, based on past learning, thinking, or biology.

5. **Normalize**. Make sense of your client's behaviors, urges, thoughts, and feelings in terms of what is true for most people.

6. **Be radically genuine**. Treat your client as an individual who is capable and competent, rather than someone who is fragile. Interact with your client in a genuine, direct manner.

5 :: Commitment Strategies

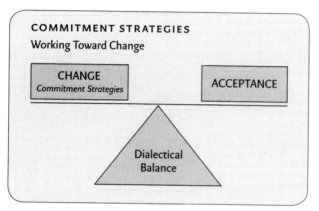

COMMITMENT STRATEGIES
Working Toward Change

CHANGE
Commitment Strategies

ACCEPTANCE

Dialectical
Balance

Commitment strategies are designed to increase motivation, which is a critical area to target with many clients. The ability to follow through on a commitment is a skill. It is important to keep in mind that most people with severe emotion dysregulation have great difficulty with the skill of following through on a commitment.

We need to assume that a client's level of commitment will fluctuate over time and will require explicit work.

At times it may be tempting to dismiss a client who is very stuck by calling her "'not motivated" or "not committed to changing." It is essential to look more deeply at what is interfering with her making a commitment or following through. Very often a person who really wants to make a change is held back by the fear of what that change would mean.

For many people, getting better may mean getting less care and attention from others, which may be frightening to contemplate. Alternatively a person may fear that he will fail if he tries to change, which will leave him even more self-blaming and hopeless.

The first step in working toward change is being explicit about the fact that your client is indeed committed to make changes. Never assume.

Be sure to ask, "Are you willing to work on this?" Or, for really hard and important goals, like stopping suicide and self-harm behaviors, you might ask, "Are you willing to do everything in your power to get through this day without harming yourself?"

> **COMMITMENT IS A SKILL**
>
> Following through on a commitment can be challenging for many clients.
>
> Assume that commitment will fluctuate over time and will require explicit work.
>
> A client who seems "not motivated" or "not committed" may actually have a strong desire to change but be held back by FEAR.

> **COMMITMENT**
> **Elicit a Commitment**
>
> Ensure that there is a clear, explicit commitment for a specific plan.
>
> *"Are you willing to . . . ?" or "Are you willing to do everything in your power . . . ?"*

Linehan (1993) outlines various commitment strategies to help you work toward receiving a firm "Yes" response. These strategies are described below.

> **COMMITMENT**
> **Pros and Cons**
>
> Weigh the advantages and disadvantages of a plan, and of making a commitment to it.
>
> Start with the *pros of the behavior*: clarify why it **makes sense** that the person has developed this habit, and discuss what the person will be giving up if he or she does change.
>
> *Cons of the behavior*: Point out the reasons to change.
>
> Look at the *pros and cons of changing* to highlight the obstacles.

An essential tool we all use in decision making is balancing pros and cons. In helping someone change impulsive behaviors like self-harm, it is often useful to inquire first about the benefits of the behavior, because this will help clarify why it makes sense that the person has developed this habit. People are often quite ashamed of liking or feeling dependent on self-harm so it is important to provide a lot of validation for these reasons, but it's important not to agree that self-harm is a good strategy. These pros also tell you what the person will be giving up if he does change, so you can start to outline the obstacles to changing.

The cons of the behavior, of course, are the reasons to change. Sometimes it can also be useful to look at not just the pros and cons of self-harming but also the pros and cons of stopping self-harm. A clear understanding of the costs of stopping can help highlight the obstacles to changing and to making a commitment to change.

COMMITMENT
Using "Reverse Psychology"
(The Devil's Advocate Strategy)

Make arguments against changing (e.g., emphasize the cons of changing).

This will increase the intensity of commitment and will prepare the client for future doubts or second thoughts.

"Why would *you want to change?"*

If it backfires, try "Generating Hope" instead.

The Devil's Advocate technique is like reverse psychology. If you argue for not making a change, for example, pointing out how hard it is or reminding the person of all the downsides of changing, many people will flip to the other side and insist that they really *do* want to change. This strategy often flows naturally from pros and cons because you have just heard about all the cons of changing. By emphasizing these you can often get a clearer picture of the opposite: the client's real reasons for wanting to change. This strategy can backfire for very tentative commitments, in which case it can be followed up with Generating Hope.

As their names imply, the Foot-in-the-Door and Door-in-the-Face strategies (Linehan, 1993) are borrowed from the persuasive techniques known in social psychology literature and used in marketing. Start by asking for a lot (Door-in-the-Face). For example, "Will you make a

---

COMMITMENT
"FOOT-IN-THE-DOOR" AND "DOOR-IN-THE-FACE"

Door-in-the-Face: Request something extremely challenging, and then revise, if needed, to something more realistic.

Foot-in-the-Door: Elicit a commitment to a small, easy plan, then gradually add more challenging requests.

---

commitment to not harm yourself at all for the next year?" If your client says, "What, are you kidding?" then bring it back to something smaller like, "Okay, how about the next week?" (Foot-in-the-Door). If he or she says, "Yes, that's possible," then keep negotiating with "How about a month?" until you find something that seems to be a realistic challenge.

Connecting to prior commitments is particularly useful later in treatment when the client appears to have forgotten the commitments made at the start. For instance, if a client keeps changing the subject when a relationship conflict comes up, one might say, "Hey, I thought you

---

COMMITMENT
Connect to Prior Commitments

Remind the client of commitments made earlier in treatment in order to:
    Strengthen a commitment that was made previously
    Help the client recall the pros of commitment

"But I thought you said you wanted to . . . "

---

told me it was a really high priority for you to reduce the conflict in your relationships." This may provide a starting point for figuring out whether that commitment needs to be reexamined or what obstacles are coming up. Here's a hint: Check to see if fear is the obstacle.

COMMITMENT
Highlight the Freedom of Choice

Highlight the client's freedom to choose his or her actions as well as the consequences of his or her choices:
   Increase the client's sense of empowerment.
   Strengthen belief that there are no other ways to achieve goals.

"You are free to decide not to change; however, the consequences are . . ."

Highlighting the freedom to choose and the consequence of a client's choice is a method of sidestepping a power struggle. This strategy may come up when a client says, "Do I *have* to?" to which you might be inclined to say, "Well, yes, if you want to get better, this *is* what you have to do."

Unfortunately, although that may be true, it is likely to elicit a more rebellious response like, "Well, I don't care. I can't and I won't do it." Highlighting the freedom to choose helps avoid that sort of polarization. In response to "Do I *have* to try out the skills?" one could say, "No, you don't, but I've got to tell you, they're the best ideas I have for how to stop blowing up at people and losing relationships."

Hope is essential to keeping commitments and making change. Many clients become easily discouraged, feel hopeless, and blame

COMMITMENT
Generate a Sense of Hope

Express your beliefs that the client is capable of change and
can commit to following through on action in order to:
Counteract the client's hopelessness
Counteract the client's fear of failure or humiliation

"I really believe that together we can figure this out."

themselves when things don't work out. Such clients require a lot of
encouragement. To be effective, cheerleading needs to be offered in a
heartfelt, meaningful way. You can't just say, "Don't worry, it'll be alright."
You need to express your belief more genuinely: "I really believe in you. I
have every confidence that you can do this and I'm going to be with you
every step of the way."

COMMITMENT
Troubleshoot Obstacles to Following Through on Goals

After eliciting a commitment, troubleshoot what obstacles could arise
that would interfere with following through on goals in order to:
Prepare for challenges
Problem solve in advance

*"What obstacles might interfere with your ability to follow through
on your goals?"*

Once you have elicited a commitment to a task, it is crucial to troubleshoot obstacles to following through on goals. What are all the factors that could interfere with the person following through on the plan? You may ask, "Can you foresee any obstacles to following through with your commitment?" You may also know from previous experience that various obstacles are likely to arise. This is the opportunity to discuss those barriers and solve the problems before they occur. Common obstacles to completing a task between sessions (e.g., practicing a skill) include forgetting, getting overwhelmed emotionally, getting physically sick, or changing one's mind and losing the sense of commitment. You and the client can brainstorm ways to ensure that the task gets done even in the face of each potential obstacle.

6 :: Distress Tolerance, AVIS–R Skills Coaching Protocol, and Solving the "Real" Problem

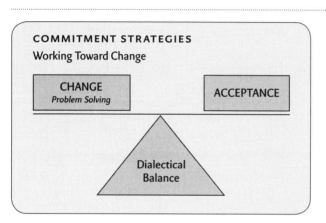

COMMITMENT STRATEGIES
Working Toward Change

CHANGE
Problem Solving

ACCEPTANCE

Dialectical Balance

Once you have elicited a commitment to work on specific problems, you and your client can start to solve the problems that brought him or her to treatment.

The first task is to figure out the real essence of the problematic behavior that you're trying to eliminate. Self-harm, as with many other impulsive behaviors, is usually a means to solve another problem. Although self-harm itself is a problem, often people harm themselves because they want to reduce emotional pain or because they have difficulties communicating directly with others. So the task with your client is to sort out the core problem that is leading him to engage in these behaviors and then to come up with a solution to address the underlying issue. For example, if the client tends to cut when he is anxious, you would identify overwhelming anxiety as the "real" problem to be solved.

Another essential element of problem solving when you are trying to help someone not harm herself is ensuring her environment is safe. When a very impulsive client is overwhelmed by an urge to harm herself, she is likely to turn to whatever object is nearest. For a problem behavior like self-harm, it could be, for example, that your client might harm herself with specific objects such as razors or knives or other instruments, and those objects may be readily available in her home. The closer these objects are, the higher the risk that they will be used during a crisis.

Of course, if the objects are visible, they can also serve as reminders of self-harm, so they can increase a client's risk directly by cuing an association with relief. So one of the things you're going to want to do is to make sure that your clients get rid of all those objects so those objects don't trigger thoughts of self-harm.

PROBLEM SOLVING

Identify the core problem: Figure out the core problem that self-harm or impulsive behaviors are attempting to solve (e.g., emotional pain).

Increase environmental safety: Decrease triggering cues and remove access to what the client uses to self-harm (e.g., get rid of sharp objects).

Use distress tolerance skills: Cope with self-harm urges or intense distress.

DISTRESS TOLERANCE SKILLS

> **DISTRESS TOLERANCE SKILLS**
>
> These skills are used to help people tolerate emotions and urges that are overwhelming and to *avoid* engaging in problematic impulsive behaviors that can be harmful.
>
> *Remember that distress tolerance skills are not designed to resolve problems or eliminate pain.*

Another thing that you're going to want to focus on is how your clients can tolerate really intense urges to engage in problematic behaviors. Distress tolerance skills are strategies that you can teach your clients to help them take the edge off of really intense emotions. They are strategies that can be used to help them get through difficult times without making the situation worse.

You are also going to want to teach your clients that distress tolerance skills don't eliminate pain because, unfortunately, even though we may want to eliminate painful emotions, we usually can't. Sometimes situations arise that are painful and in those situations, the measure of success is managing through very intense emotions without engaging in harmful impulsive behaviors.

There are many different ways to tolerate distress. We will mention a few of them here. One very helpful way to distract from heightened arousal, in order to reduce physiological arousal, is to hold something very cold. You can coach your client to hold ice packs on his skin or to jump in an ice-cold shower. The sensation of cold helps the individual to shift his attention away from his distress. It's hard to be focused on self-harm when you're standing in an ice-cold shower.

TEACHING DISTRESS TOLERANCE SKILLS

Coach clients to reduce distress from painful emotions with some specific distress tolerance skills, including distraction, engaging in activities, and relaxation.

Intense sensation of cold temperature: Hold an ice cube or ice pack, take an ice-cold shower

Exercise: Walking, jogging, bicycling

Mindful breathing: Reduces hyperventilation and body tension

Clients need to practice these skills when NOT in distress.

Another strategy is to distract by engaging in activities such as exercise. This can involve going for a fast-paced walk, jogging, or riding a bicycle. Finally, slow, deep breathing can help promote relaxation and can reduce intense arousal. All of these skills are helpful because they can reduce the intensity of negative emotion.

Coach your client to practice these skills at times when he is not in distress, because, like any other new skill, you've got to practice a lot before you try to use a new skill in a difficult situation.

AVIS-R SKILLS COACHING PROTOCOL

CHARLIE SWENSON'S AVIS-R SKILLS COACHING PROTOCOL

1. ATTEND to the client and the problem.
2. ASSESS the problem behavior.
3. VALIDATE the pain that led to the problem.
4. VALIDATE the difficulty of trying to change/using skills.
5. INVITE the client to use a skill and give a rationale.
6. INSTRUCT the client on how to use the skill.
7. SHOW or model the skill.
8. SEE the client use the skill.
9. REINFORCE and praise the adaptive behavior.
10. REVIEW to get feedback on the helpfulness of the new skill/behavior.

So far we have looked at how to work with someone who is calm during your meetings and who talks about being emotionally dysregulated in the rest of her life. But how do you react when your client's affect is dysregulated right in front of you? The psychiatrist Dr. Charlie Swenson developed this skills coaching protocol specifically for front-line staff who deal with dysregulated people. It's a 10-step protocol with the acronym AVIS-R. There are two steps per letter.

A   The first A is a reminder to **attend** to the person. Focus only on that person and really try to get her attention. This could be done simply through eye contact or saying her name.

The second A is for **assess**. This may be as simple as saying, "Hey, what's going on?"

V Validation is so important that it gets two steps in this protocol. First, you **validate the pain** that the person is in: "Oh, my, that is really upsetting" or "I see why you're completely overwhelmed."

Next you **validate how hard it is to try responding differently** such as, "It's really hard to try something new when you're this upset." So, first, you validate the pain and then you validate the difficulty of changing.

I The next step is to **invite** the person to use a skill. This is essentially the same as eliciting a commitment. You are checking out that she actually wants your help before you give it. Giving a rationale is important too. Why *would* she want to try something new right now? Well, probably if you can help her calm down you'll then be able to problem solve together. Or maybe she is in the midst of an urge to drink and needs reminding about why this was a goal in the first place. For example, "I'd like to help you get through this without drinking so you don't miss work tomorrow and risk getting fired."

Presuming that she has agreed to receive your help, you can go on to **instruct** or suggest a skill to use in the moment, name it, and give a brief explanation. Depending on the client and where you are, you might suggest holding ice, doing jumping jacks, taking a bath, listening to music, watching TV, or being mindful of breathing.

S The first S is **showing** the client the skill, which may not always be possible. It is most relevant for skills that can be done together like breathing, progressive muscle relaxation, jumping jacks, or making self-validating statements. Sharing a personal example is also often helpful.

Seeing the client do the skill is also mainly applicable when it's a skill you can practice together.

R   The first R is to provide **positive reinforcement** in the form of praise for whatever steps the person has taken toward attempting a skill or being willing to try it out. Examples are "Nice job, good for you" or "You did really well with that."

The second R is **review**. Take a moment to get feedback, such as "Was this helpful?" If it makes sense in the situation, you might even do a detailed review looking at what might help even more.

SOLVING THE "REAL" PROBLEM

> **SOLVING THE "REAL" PROBLEM**
>
> The work of treatment is to reduce emotional and behavioral dysregulation and increase effective coping behaviors.
>
> This can be done once the client is willing, committed, and regulated.

In the clinical vignette that you viewed, when Ashley settled from her dysregulated state she and Shelley were able to turn their attention to what set off her painful emotions and her impulse to quit her job. They focused on helping to reduce the intensity of the client's pain and helping her not to react to it in impulsive, damaging ways.

> **SOLVING THE "REAL" PROBLEM**
> **Starting a Behavioral Chain Analysis**
>
> Elicit the client's description of the event, maintaining a focus on the emotions that she was experiencing.
>
> Identify and problem solve the links in the chain surrounding the problem behavior = behavioral chain analysis.

Shelley started by listening to Ashley nonjudgmentally as she described the problem, paying close attention to which specific emotions Ashley was experiencing. Shelley then started a behavioral chain analysis to identify the links in the chain surrounding the problematic behavior (e.g., the client's plan to quit her job).

The first step is to be clear on what the **problem** actually is—which specific behavior is being analyzed. Focus on a specific instance of a problematic behavior that the client has agreed to work on in treatment, such as high urges to self-harm or an angry outburst. The next step is to identify the **prompting event**—the moment or incident that started the client on the chain toward the problem behavior.

Of utmost importance is examining exactly how the prompting event and the problem behavior are connected. These **links** may include many different thoughts, decisions, emotions, urges, or actions. For instance, on the surface there may not be an obvious connection between a relationship breakup and suicidal urges. Examining all the links may

SOLVING THE "REAL" PROBLEM
Steps in a Behavioral Chain Analysis

Clarify which **problematic behavior** is being analyzed (e.g., self-harm or an angry outburst).

Identify the **prompting event** that started the "chain" toward the problem behavior.

Examine the **links in the chain**: all elements that connect the prompting event to the problem behavior (e.g., thoughts, decisions, emotions, urges, actions).

Identify **consequences** that may reinforce the problem behavior (e.g., relief, more soothing attention from others).

reveal that the client was feeling intense hurt and anger and then she had a thought like, "I shouldn't be feeling this way," followed by another thought, "I can't stand feeling this way," followed next by the thought that suicide would be a way to stop the pain.

SOLVING THE REAL PROBLEM
Solution Analysis

Collaboratively work on identifying possible **solutions** to the problematic behaviors that are identified in the behavioral chain analysis.
    This may include brainstorming skills to tolerate pain, working on challenging dysfunctional beliefs, and increasing interpersonal effectiveness.

The responses that follow the problem behavior are also very important. Problematic **consequences** could reinforce impulsive behavior or
punish desired behavior. Problematic consequences of self-harm usually
include intense relief from the underlying painful emotions and may also
include attention or caring from other people or a sense that the client
has been able to communicate how much pain she is in. More helpful
consequences could include disappointment or a renewed commitment
to using skills instead of self-harm.

Once some important links have been identified, solutions can be
generated. For instance, the client and the therapist can brainstorm
ways to tolerate or reduce intense pain other than suicide. They can also
directly challenge the thoughts that "she should not feel this way" or that
"she really cannot stand it."

7 :: Concluding Remarks

WITH EMOTIONALLY DYSREGULATED CLIENTS . . .

- Stay compassionate and validating, while pushing for change.
- Elicit a commitment to specific goals (i.e., pros and cons, be the devil's advocate, highlight the freedom to choose, generate hope).
- Teach distress tolerance skills.
- Increase environmental safety.
- Identify and solve underlying problems.

The ideas in this learning guide will help you in your work with clients who struggle with emotional dysregulation and impulsive behaviors such as self-harm. The key ingredients are focusing on validation and acceptance while at the same time helping your client to make changes. Don't try to change behaviors that your client hasn't yet agreed to work on. Ensure that you first start by clarifying your client's commitment to address specific goals in treatment. To elicit a commitment it can be helpful to use some of Linehan's DBT strategies such as pros and cons, playing devil's advocate, and highlighting the freedom to choose. In your work, remember to coach clients on skills, remove environmental cues or triggers where possible, and identify and solve the core problem (avoidance of painful emotion) that motivates impulsive behaviors.

Lesson Plans

(See Appendix C for answers.)

LESSON PLAN #1

Watch "Explanation of the biosocial theory," "Explanation of Validation," "Validation Role Play #1."

A. Discussion

    i.   Use the biosocial theory: Think about a client you are currently working with who elicits strong feelings in you (e.g., anxiety, hopelessness, frustration). In one nonjudgmental sentence, describe the behavior that prompts your emotion. Then, referring to the biosocial theory, explain why it makes perfect sense that this person behaves the way he or she does. If you do not have enough information to know, ask the client at your next meeting about his or her early temperament and how caregivers had responded to his or her emotions. If you are still stumped, get input from colleagues.

2. Figure out validating statements in response to the following client statements:
    a. "What's the point?"
    b. [after you have been late for the last two meetings:] "It's obvious you don't care about me—you've been late for our last two meetings."
    c. [when you have *not* actually been late for the last two meetings, although you have been in the past:] "It's obvious you don't care about me—you've been late for our last two meetings."
    d. "You're not helping me at all."
    e. "I wish I wasn't so out of control. I'm such a loser."
    f. "Self-harm is the only thing that helps me in my life; without it I would be dead."

B. Experiential Tasks

1. Review the six ways of validating as presented in the DVD and accompanying booklet:
    • Appear interested
    • Paraphrase

- Mind read
- Make sense based on history
- Normalize what is true for all
- Be radically genuine

2. Pair up with a colleague to discuss an experience you have had with a client. Tell your colleague about a difficult session you had recently: include your feelings and thoughts, as well as what you actually said to the client. Ask your colleague to respond to you only by using each different way of validating, to demonstrate that he or she hears and understands what you are saying. As often as possible, your colleague should point out what is normal about what you thought and felt about your client, and he or she should offer explanations for why your reactions make perfect sense. Then switch roles.

3. Pair up with a colleague to role play a client situation. You can pretend to be your client; ask your colleague to play the therapist/counselor/social worker, etc. Act out a recent conversation you had with a client who was feeling angry or afraid or having another intense emotion. As you pretend to be your client and quote what she or he said, have your colleague find something valid in everything you say and reflect that back to you. Afterward, think about which of your colleague's statements made you feel understood, soothed, and/or connected to him or her. Discuss your reactions with each other and then switch roles.

C. Homework

1. The biosocial theory: For any clients for whom you do not have enough history from their early life to understand why it is only logical that they turned out the way they did, *ask them* about (1) their early temperament and (2) their caregivers' responses to their emotions.

    The early temperament can be elicited with questions like, "What did your caregivers tell you about what kind of infant you were?" (e.g., calm, happy, easy to feed, easy to settle). Emotionally sensitive infants are often more fussy, colicky, irregular, and harder to soothe. It can also be helpful to ask questions like, "What were you like as a young child? Were you sociable or shy? Excited or nervous to do new things? Did you have temper tantrums?" Emotionally sensitive children are often painfully shy, overwhelmed when separated from caregivers, or have out-of-control temper outbursts.

    Write out a short paragraph to yourself explaining why the client could not have turned out any other way. Here is an example, written by a therapist who was frustrated by a client who continued to self-harm despite learning and using distress tolerance skills: "My client was an extremely sensitive child who had much stronger emotional reactions than her siblings. She consistently received the message from her parents that she was overreacting and that her responses were not just wrong but irritating and embarrassing to them. Given that she had this sensitive temperament and invalidating environment, it is no wonder that she now panics whenever she has an emotion, and she tries to get rid of the feeling as fast as possible (in her case, by drinking or harming herself)."

Read this paragraph to yourself in moments when it is hard to be compassionate toward your client.

2. Have a pad of paper with you for several client meetings or phone calls. Focus on one way of validating at a time and write yourself a note each time you use it. For example, for a few sessions, focus on mind reading and accurately name the emotion if the client doesn't do so. Write it down each time you name an emotion.

3. With your clients, see if you can notice the urge to give advice, reassure, apologize, or explain your intent. Before doing any of those things, stop, take a breath, and validate the client. Then carry on.

4. Notice if you have thoughts during or after client sessions like "That was totally the wrong thing to say," "How could I have been so stupid?" or "I'm a terrible therapist/counselor/case worker, etc." Practice self-validation by going through the following steps.

    a. Notice that these statements are self-judgmental thoughts, not facts. For example, "I just had the thought 'I'm a terrible therapist.'"

    b. Validate that frustration is a normal emotional response to judgments. For example, "This feeling is a perfectly normal reaction to my judgments about having made a therapeutic mistake."

c. Nonjudgmentally name what you did that you feel badly about. For example, "When my client withdrew in our session today, I lost my patience with her and told her in an irritated tone that she needed to collaborate with me. I also did not validate her experience."

d. Find something that makes sense about what you did. Even if it was not desirable, what was perfectly normal or understandable about it? For example, "Much as I want to be perfect and always stay patient with my clients, it is in fact perfectly normal to have an off day sometimes. I am quite stressed this week, behind on deadlines, not sleeping well, and also specifically frustrated with this client because I am worried about her lack of progress."

e. Next time you meet this client, keep these steps in mind and validate your own worry and frustration before saying anything to her.

LESSON PLAN #2

Watch "Explanation of Commitment Strategies," "Commitment Strategies Role Play #2," "Explanation of Problem Solving," and "Problem-Solving Role Play #3." (Identify the real problem [underlying emotion]; increase environmental safety; distress tolerance skills)

A. Discussion

1. Watch the commitment role play (without looking at the transcription) and identify the validation strategies that are used in it.

2. Watch the problem-solving role play (without looking at the transcription) and identify the commitment strategies that are used in it.

    Read the following scenario and come up with examples of the Devil's Advocate, Freedom to Choose, and Foot-in-the-Door/Door-in-the-Face exercises that would help get a commitment to staying alive.

    Therapist: I'd really love to work with you. You have several really important goals that I really think I can help you with. My only concern is you have mentioned thinking about killing yourself. I'm not clear how it makes sense to work on all these things unless I know you're going to stick around. After all, we won't get anywhere if my goal is to help you build a better life but your goal is to stop living. Are you on board with the goal of not killing yourself for at least the next year (or duration of treatment)?

    Client: I don't know, I mean, if I decide to do it I just might. Who can say what'll happen?

3. Reflect on how you and your friends or family tolerate distress in your own lives. What distracting activities are effective for people around you? What other methods do people use (e.g., physical self-soothing; not giving into urges by reminding yourself of what's really important in life; just feeling and expressing the pain without acting on it; accessing social or spiritual support, and many more)? Remember these methods when you work with your clients.

B. Experiential Tasks

1. Role play: Have a colleague pretend that he or she strongly believes that the best way to lose a few pounds is to completely stop eating anything at all for the next 2 weeks. Try to elicit a commitment to consider another solution. Be direct and genuine while staying respectful and validating of their opinion. Focus on the Pros and Cons, Freedom to Choose, and Devil's Advocate techniques.

2. Obtain an ice pack or pieces of ice wrapped in a paper towel. Hold the ice to your temples and forehead for about 30 seconds. (Do not do this if you have heart or blood pressure problems.) What do you notice? Pay attention to your thoughts, emotions, and physical sensations.

3. Notice the power of visual reminders. If you are trying to eat fewer sweets, what happens if you leave a box of your favorite cookies on the counter? If you are trying to remember to take

vitamins, what happens if you put the bottle next to your toothbrush? Or if you are trying to get to the gym more often, will putting a sign on your closet door remind you of how good you feel after you do so? Plan an experiment this week in which you use visual reminders to help yourself remember to do something. (Alternatively, remove visual reminders to help yourself stop doing something.) Share this experience the next time you talk to a client about removing self-harm implements, cleaning out drugs or alcohol from their house, or making signs to remind them to practice coping skills.

C. Homework

1. Review your client list and identify those who have a history of emotion dysregulation and impulsive behavior (especially self-harm and suicide attempts). If you aren't sure about their history, ask direct questions. For those clients with self-harm or suicide attempts, use commitment strategies to gain a firm commitment to eliminate self-harm or to make a wholehearted commitment to staying alive "no matter what" (e.g., even if past stressful circumstances occur again). For those clients with other impulsive behaviors, use commitment strategies to strengthen their commitment to stopping or reducing these behaviors.

2. For your clients who have harmed themselves within the past few months or continue to have strong urges, coach them to get rid of any cues, implements, or pill stashes in their environment.

Use lots of validation and commitment strategies.

3. If you expect your client to complete a task or do some sort of homework before the next session, elicit a commitment to do so, and then spend a few minutes troubleshooting. For example, "What could come up that would get in the way of your following through on this task? Say you forget, you get busy/stressed, you get sick, your car breaks down, your child care arrangements fall through. Are you willing to ensure you get it done even if those things happen? If so, how will you ensure it (e.g., problem solve in advance; make backup plans)?"

4. Teach distress tolerance skills to at least one client. Help him to make a list of 20 to 30 activities he could realistically do during a crisis, and encourage him to write down how many minutes he could do each one. Hint: he may benefit from separate lists for mild, moderate, or really severe crises.

LESSON PLAN #3
Watch "Coaching Protocol Explanation," "Behavioral Chain Analysis Explanation," and "Avis-R Coaching Protocol Role Play #4."

A. Discussion
1. Review the 10 steps of the AVIS-R protocol in responding to the following situation. In the hallway you bump into your client Jane, who is in tears. When she sees you, she says, "My boyfriend

just broke up with me and I'm so upset I can't even breathe!" She starts to hyperventilate. [Hint: Some of the steps are very short, e.g., half a sentence.]

2. Watch the Problem-Solving Role Play #3. The section captioned "gathering details of the most recent self-harm incident" is a mini–behavioral chain analysis. Identify which components of the behavioral chain analysis are mentioned in the role play. What information is needed for a more thorough analysis? Indicate which questions need to be asked and imagine some possible answers.

B. Experiential Tasks

1. Practice completing a behavioral chain analysis about yourself. Consider focusing on the last time you did something you regretted. [Hint: If the behavior was avoiding something (e.g., getting to the gym), or being late (e.g., for work), clarify the links by asking yourself questions like "When did I realize I was going to be late/not get to the gym?" "At what point did I decide not to go?" "When would I have had to get out of the house to be on time?" "Did I make any decisions that ensured I wouldn't make it (e.g., stopping for a coffee on the way in, or checking one more email; going home to eat before the gym and then feeling too sluggish/comfortable)?" There may not be an obvious prompting event per se, but you may be able to pinpoint the first link in the chain instead.]

Once you have completed the behavioral chain analysis, review the ineffective links. Which links could you change? What is needed to change them (willingness to get up earlier, acceptance of the need to get to bed earlier, stronger commitment to go to the gym, tolerating the anxiety of leaving things undone, planning to pack a snack between work and the gym, etc.)?

2. Role play the AVIS-R protocol with a colleague using this scenario:

During your meeting with her, Sally says she is feeling fine now but has been spending most of her nights ruminating about her boyfriend because she is so frustrated with his inconsistency and lack of communication. She is pretty sure the same thing will happen tonight, especially if he calls. She predicts she will again not be able to stop thinking about it and will probably drink a whole bottle of wine to make the thoughts stop. Despite her anger with her boyfriend, she wants your help figuring out how to cope without drinking.

C. Homework

1. Use the AVIS-R protocol the next time you have a dysregulated client. This can be applied to many situations, including clients experiencing anxiety, shame, or in-session withdrawal (i.e., they don't have to be angry or out of control).

2.   Teach a client how to do a behavioral chain analysis for a problem behavior she wants to stop doing. Work together on identifying which links can be changed and what skills are needed to change them.

LESSON PLAN #4
Consolidation and Clinical Applications

Case #1

Lucy is a 20-year-old college student who has been struggling with binge drinking since her early teens. She is seeking therapy because, for the past 3 months, she has been impulsively missing class so often that she is worried she might get kicked out of college. She says she intends to go to classes but different things happen that continually result in her missing them—sometimes she is too hungover, sometimes she is so absorbed in an argument with her boyfriend that she forgets about class, sometimes she is in such a good mood that she hangs out with friends instead because "going to class is more of a downer," and sometimes she is so overwhelmed with the things going on in her social circle that she stays home in tears. She is intent on finishing her diploma so she can become a medical lab technician, so she readily agrees to work with you on regulating her emotions better to ensure she attends her classes.

She was raised by her mother, who was 18 when Lucy was born. She described her mother as an "alcoholic with a temper" and said that she was kept up at night as a child because her mother was always fighting with various boyfriends. Sometimes she had to stay home from school because her mother was not awake in time to help her get ready. She remembers being a feisty, rebellious child with strong opinions and intense reactions. She recalls her mother rolling her eyes and telling her she was "always overreacting" when she got upset about things.

A. Discussion

1. Imagine that Lucy is your client and said to you, "I can't understand why I turned out like this—why can't I control my emotions and just go to class?" Devise an answer to her question by using the biosocial theory (i.e., explaining that she turned out the way she did because of the interaction of biological tendencies with an invalidating environment).

2. Imagine that Lucy came to a therapy session and said, "I just can't believe my friend! I've learned my lesson—I'll never trust her again. Can you believe this—last night we went out, and she starts flirting and dancing with my boyfriend! She was all over him! Unbelievable!! I'm never speaking to her again." Review the six ways of validating. Then give an example of each one in response to her story.

3. Imagine that after a few weeks of therapy Lucy said, "I know I'm supposed to work on getting to class more, but tomorrow is my

best friend's birthday and I'm going to spend it preparing this amazing surprise party for her—she'll be so happy!!"

    a. Imagine responding to her, first with normalizing validation, and then with validation in the context of her biology and history.

    b. Give examples of how you might use the following commitment strategies to help strengthen her commitment to attending class:

        i. Devil's Advocate

        ii. Freedom to Choose and the Absence of Alternatives

        iii. Pros and Cons

        iv. Connecting to Prior Commitments

B. Experiential Tasks

Case #2

Dave is a 40-year-old bookstore owner who presented for therapy a few months after his second wife left him. He acknowledges he has always been volatile and moody, and his 8-year relationship with his wife was marked by intense conflict and several separations. He has been feeling "out of control" since she left, with unpredictable moods, anger outbursts, and overwhelming bouts of guilt, panic, self-hatred, and loneliness. He states that these emotions have been so unbearable that he can get relief from them only by superficially cutting his arms. He has been cutting himself 3 or 4 times weekly for about 3 months.

Prior to this he had not deliberately injured himself since his teens. He made two suicide attempts by overdosing on 50 to 60 pills of Tylenol in his early 20s, but he has not been suicidal since then.

1. Ask a colleague to role play as Dave while you role play as his therapist.
    a. Have a discussion with Dave about his self-harm:
        i.   Explain to him the "real problem" underlying his self-harm behavior.
        ii. Assuming Dave agrees to eliminate self-harm, help him ensure that his environment is safe.
        iii. Teach Dave some distress tolerance skills he can use when he is overwhelmed with emotions.

    b. One day, half an hour before his therapy session, Dave receives a phone call from his wife about their divorce settlement. He loses his temper on the phone and hangs up on her. In session he is initially agitated and shifting about in his seat; in the next 2–3 minutes he escalates to crying, hyperventilating, and moaning, interspersed with making choked statements about being "a worthless piece of crap who doesn't deserve to be on the planet." In a role play, use the AVIS-R protocol to coach him to focus on his breath so that he can be more emotionally regulated.

    c. After a month in therapy, despite moving the sharp scissors out of the bedside drawer, Dave continues to cut himself about twice weekly. Most recently he woke up early after a poor night's sleep and was ruminating about his last meeting with the divorce lawyer. He believed the lawyer—who reminded him of his wife—hated him and wasn't really on his side. That morning he shaved himself with a safety razor as usual, and then it occurred to him to use this to scrape some skin off of his arm, which he did, until it bled. In a role play, conduct a behavioral chain analysis of the self-harm and collaboratively brainstorm ways that Dave could work on (a) being less vulnerable to harming himself and (b) using more skills to manage his thoughts, emotions, and urges.

Quiz

(See Appendix C for answers.)

Please complete the following questions on Dialectical Behavior Therapy to the best of your knowledge. For the multiple choice questions, there is only ONE correct response for each question—choose the best answer to each question.

1. What are the three features of an emotionally sensitive temperament?

    • _____

    • _____

    • _____

2. What are the three theories or philosophies that form the theoretical basis of DBT?

- _____
- _____
- _____

A client is consistently 20 minutes late for your session. At your fourth meeting she is again 20 minutes late. You know that she has trouble stopping whatever she is doing before she leaves home, such as school homework, laundry, or talking to a friend on the phone. She is clearly embarrassed by how difficult it is to get the timing right and apologizes very sincerely: "I'm so sorry. I know this is really wasting your time. It's really important to me to make it on time, and I am trying my hardest."

3. The following are all potential DBT therapist responses. Which of the responses illustrate a dialectical statement?

   A. "I just realized I may have been contributing to the problem by extending our meetings beyond the hour I have scheduled."
   B. "That's great that you're trying so hard to figure this out! I'm glad that you are so committed to these appointments."
   C. "I can see how important it is to you to get here on time, and I know you are not coming late on purpose."
   D. "I am confident that if we keep at it, we'll be able to figure this out and get you here on time."

E. "Clearly this is painful to talk about, and it's really important! Let's sort out what needs to happen so you are for sure here on time next week."

a. E
b. A and B
c. C
d. B, C, and D
e. C and E

Anne is a 25-year-old woman who is seeing a therapist/counselor because she tends to respond to overwhelming painful emotions by harming herself, drinking alcohol, or binge eating. After 3 months of therapy, she has been able to stop self-harming, but her binge eating has increased from sporadically to about 5 times weekly. She and her therapist have focused their fourth month of treatment on reducing binge eating, but she continues to binge about 5 times every week. At the start of their fifth month working together, Anne comes to the session and says, "I binged 5 times again last week. Clearly I'm never going to get this—I guess I've accomplished as much as I'm going to in therapy, so I might as well quit."

The following four questions provide potential therapist responses to the above scenario. Identify which type of validation each question uses.

4. The therapist says, "You sound utterly frustrated—and pretty hopeless, too!"

a. Reflecting
b. Mind reading
c. Validating based on history
d. Normalizing
e. Cheerleading

5. The therapist says, "It makes perfect sense that you would be struggling to change this behavior—this is a deeply ingrained habit! I mean, you've been using bingeing to regulate your emotions for over 10 years."
   a. Reflecting
   b. Mind reading
   c. Validating based on history
   d. Normalizing
   e. Cheerleading

6. The therapist says, "Listen, we have been working together for a few months now, and I have learned that you are an amazingly strong and determined person. I have every confidence in your ability to figure this out, and together I believe we can do it!"
   a. Reflecting
   b. Mind reading
   c. Validating based on history
   d. Normalizing
   e. Cheerleading

7. The therapist says, "Hey, of course you are having an urge to quit—this is exactly the response you tend to have when you hit an obstacle: your brain looks for ways to escape or avoid."
   a. Reflecting
   b. Mind reading
   c. Validating based on history
   d. Normalizing
   e. Cheerleading

Use the same case example above for the following four questions:

8. The therapist says, "You have a point—in fact, you've done very well to stop self-harming, and after all, bingeing is less dangerous to your life and limb. Maybe it makes sense to stop now." Which commitment strategy is this an example of?
   a. Devil's Advocate
   b. Foot-in-the-Door/Door-in-the-Face
   c. Connect to Prior Commitments
   d. Highlight the Freedom to Choose
   e. Generate Hope

9. The therapist says, "Hey, you know, you could quit now. You've done well so far and I can see how frustrated you've become. You could decide to keep bingeing—I think you'd have a tough life in terms of continuing to hide them and your other disordered eating habits from the people close to you, but, really, it's up to you in the end." Which commitment strategy is this an example of?

    a. Devil's Advocate

    b. Foot-in-the-Door/Door-in-the-Face

    c. Connect to Prior Commitments

    d. Highlight the Freedom to Choose

    e. Generate Hope

10. The therapist says, "Hmm, this is interesting: I thought you told me last month that getting your eating habits under control was absolutely your highest priority now and that you were going to do everything in your power to figure out how to stop bingeing." Which commitment strategy is this an example of?

    a. Devil's Advocate

    b. Foot-in-the-Door/Door-in-the-Face

    c. Connect to Prior Commitments

    d. Highlight the Freedom to Choose

    e. Generate Hope

11. The therapist says, "Listen, we have ourselves a really tough problem here. Clearly a month just hasn't been enough time to fully figure it out. I really think we've just got to keep plugging away at it—over time we will be able to solve this! Let's analyze one of the binges from this week and really take a close look at what's getting in the way of using skills instead of bingeing." Which commitment strategy is this an example of?

    a. Devil's Advocate

    b. Foot-in-the-Door/Door-in-the-Face

    c. Connect to Prior Commitments

d. Highlight the Freedom to Choose

e. Generate Hope

12. Mary comes into her second meeting sobbing and overwhelmed. She is almost unable to speak but manages to tell you she has been evicted from her apartment this morning and then discovered her wallet had been stolen. She curls up in the chair and wails loudly. Which of the following responses is most consistent with the DBT coaching protocol?

a. "Oh, Mary, what a situation! Let's figure out where you can live. Have you called the police about your wallet?"

b. "Mary, this is dreadful! How could you not be completely overwhelmed!? Here's an ice pack—hold on to that now and bring your full attention to it."

c. "Mary, Mary, you'll be okay. You'll get through this. It'll all work itself out. I'm here with you. It'll be okay."

d. "I'll help you with problem solving just as soon as you're calm enough. Take your time. Let me know when you're ready."

e. "Breathe, Mary! You've got to take some deep breaths, so you can calm down and we can talk about what's going on."

A therapist and his client, Fred, are working on decreasing the number of incidents of impulsive sexual activity Fred engages in per week. In the course of focusing on the most recent occurrence of this behavior in the last session, the therapist learns the following pieces of information:

A. Fred was out with friends in the afternoon and had four drinks.

B. Over dinner with his parents, his mother told him he should be happy about the new job he just got, since it won't last long, given his history of short-lived employment. In response, he blew up and swore at her.

C. He went out to a bar and had three more drinks.

D. At the bar, he asked a woman if she wanted to go home with him.

E. On the way to his apartment, she asked if he had ever had any sexually transmitted diseases and he lied and said no (he has had herpes outbreaks in the past).

F. She did not insist that he use a condom.

G. They had unprotected sex.

H. After having sex, he felt soothed and relaxed for several hours.

I. Now that he is talking about it, he feels overwhelmed with shame for having "messed up," for lying to the woman, and for possibly exposing her to herpes.

13. During the session the therapist and client collaboratively complete a behavioral chain analysis. What is the problem behavior?

a. Lying about herpes

b. Drinking alcohol in the afternoon

c. Having impulsive sex

d. Fighting with his parents

e. Feeling overwhelmed with shame

14. What was the prompting event?
    a. Lying about herpes
    b. Drinking alcohol in the afternoon
    c. Having impulsive sex
    d. Fighting with his parents
    e. Feeling overwhelmed with shame

15. What made him vulnerable?
    a. Lying about herpes
    b. Drinking alcohol in the afternoon
    c. Having impulsive sex
    d. Fighting with his parents
    e. Feeling overwhelmed with shame

16. Which of the following were links in the chain?
    a. C, D, E, and F
    b. C, F, G, and I
    c. A and C
    d. H and I
    e. B, D, and E

17. Which of the following were problematic consequences?
    a. C, D, E, and F
    b. C, F, G, and I
    c. A and C
    d. H and I
    e. B, D, and E

18. From a DBT perspective, which of the following may represent the "real" meaning of the problem underlying his sexual impulsivity?
    a. He is unable to control his impulses.
    b. He has a sexual addiction.
    c. He has unresolved anger toward his mother.
    d. He has difficulty regulating anger and anxiety.
    e. He has alcohol dependence.

19. Which of the following assumptions about him is NOT consistent with DBT?
    a. He is doing the best he can.
    b. He needs to try harder.
    c. He has to solve his own problems.
    d. He is exploitative and manipulative.
    e. He needs to be more motivated.

A client attempts suicide by overdosing on her father's heart medication. She is admitted to the ICU at the local hospital for several days and then discharged.

Here is a short conversation at the start of her next therapy session. At each number, identify which type of strategy is being used.

Client: *I know I really let you down by taking that overdose. I let myself down too. Actually I think I'm a loser for doing it, and clearly a failure as a client—and as a person.*

Therapist: *Hey, you sound really self-judgmental right now.*
[question 20]

Client: *I guess.*

Therapist: *When those self-judgments come to mind, how about just letting them go and gently bringing your focus to your breathing?* [question 21]

Client: [sighs] *Okay.*

Therapist: *Are you willing to drop the judgments and work with me on figuring out how to do everything in your power to avoid overdosing again?* [question 22]

Client: *Yes, I really want to stop doing this.*

Therapist: *Great! I'm so glad we're on the same page here.* [question 23] *So why don't you start by telling me what was going on that day before you overdosed?* [question 24]

20. Which option best describes this strategy?
    a. Validation
    b. Commitment
    c. Problem solving
    d. Skills coaching
    e. None of the above

21. Which option best describes this strategy?
    a. Validation
    b. Commitment
    c. Problem solving
    d. Skills coaching
    e. None of the above

22. Which option best describes this strategy?
    a. Validation
    b. Commitment
    c. Problem solving
    d. Skills coaching
    e. None of the above

23. Which option best describes this strategy?
    a. Validation
    b. Commitment
    c. Problem solving
    d. Skills coaching
    e. None of the above

24. Which option best describes this strategy?
    a. Validation
    b. Commitment
    c. Problem solving
    d. Skills coaching
    e. None of the above

In the second meeting a client says, "You know, I just don't think I'm ready to give up my impulsive spending. I've tried before and haven't been able to do it. Besides, I find it's the only thing in life that really gives me a thrill. I enjoy it. Let's take it off my list of goals."

25. Which option best illustrates a validating response?
    a. "Surely there are other things you find enjoyable in life. Let's figure out what else you can do that's fun besides shopping."
    b. "You're really discouraged about the prospect of changing this. You've tried before and it just seemed too hard."
    c. "You might be right that you are simply not someone who is strong or capable enough to make this kind of change."
    d. "I don't think it's that hard to change this—you should be able to get your spending under control if you really want to."
    e. "You've been able to go a whole month without overspending at all—I think that's terrific!"

26. Which of the following responses would be an effective commitment strategy?
    a. "Are you willing to do everything in your power to stop overspending?"
    b. "Could we review the most recent time you shopped impulsively?"
    c. "You seem really afraid to tackle this; I wonder if you're worried about failing?"
    d. "So why *would* you want to work on this problem with me?"
    e. "Why don't we start small and see if you can go just one week without overspending?"

27. Why would it be premature to offer a problem-solving response to this client?

a. She is not capable of getting her spending under control.

b. She has not bonded well enough with the therapist yet.

c. She is too upset to engage in a logical conversation.

d. She is not able to tolerate direct questioning.

e. She has not made a commitment to work on this behavior.

Appendix A: Role-Play Transcripts

(Refer to the enclosed DVD for the full video.)

INTRODUCTORY CLIP

C: I'm so angry. I'm so angry at that jerk. You know what? I'm going to quit my job. I'm going to quit because he just . . . it's not even my fault that that thing happened. It's not even my fault that those guys were fighting. I wasn't even serving them. You know what, I'm sick of it.

T: Ashley, one sec. Take a minute.

C: I'm going to quit. I'm just . . .

T: Ashley, I don't know what's happening but it looks pretty intense.

C: Yeah, it's intense.

T: You look really uncomfortable.

C: I'm so uncomfortable and I'm so . . . I'm just angry at that guy. He's just a jerk. I don't know why it's my fault.

T: Okay, so it sounds like a lot has happened, something happened at work and it looks pretty intense right now.

C: Yeah. I'm going to quit. Can I quit? Is that okay?

ROLE PLAY #1: VALIDATION STRATEGIES

This is the first meeting with Ashley after some initial information has been gathered. The therapist integrates validation strategies into a conversation about whether or not Ashley wants to work on self-harm.

T: Just to recap where we're at so far in our discussion, thanks a lot for your candor around your history and background . . . [**Positive Reinforcement**] and I just wanted to summarize what you've told me about the goals that you want to work on with me, just to make sure that I've got that right. So it seems like one of the most important things you wanted to talk about is relationships, because you've got a number of conflicts in relationships and that's a really important area to look at. Then emotions, you were saying sometimes you feel really out of control of your emotions and that's something you really wanted to target with me. And then we also touched a little bit on the issue of work and school maybe, or getting off disability, and that's something that you were thinking is maybe a longer-term goal, not something to tackle right away. [**Validating—Reflecting: Summarizing goals**] Have I got all that right?

C: Yeah.

T: Great. In terms of goals, one of the things I wanted to raise is, I noticed from the intake report that you've actually been self-harming quite frequently. [**Validating: Interacting in a genuine, direct manner**] [*client looks down*] How are you doing? You're actually looking pretty withdrawn right now. [**Validating—Attend to an in-session emotion**] What's up?

C: Embarrassed, I guess.

T: So it's a tough topic, eh? [**Validating—Reflecting**] Yeah, it really is for a lot of people. [**Validation—Normalizing in the context of people who self-harm**] So I'm getting the sense that there's actually quite a lot of emotion around this subject. [**Validating—Reflecting**] Is it something that you'd want to look at with me, to try to figure out other ways of coping? [**Eliciting Commitment**]

C: Yes, but I don't think you can help.

T: You're actually sounding kind of hopeless about this. [**Validation— Mind Reading**] Is that right?

C: M'hmm.

T: I'm wondering: Is this something you've actually tried to tackle before?

C: I've tried but nothing works.

T: I was just thinking, it really totally makes sense to me that you'd feel hopeless about it if you've tried to target this before and it just hasn't worked, nothing has helped. [**Validating—Making sense in terms of past experiences**]

C: M'hmm.

T: Well, I do want you to know that, although this is a very tough problem—and I think this is true for most people who self-harm: it's a really hard thing to stop doing—[**Validating—Making sense in the context of pathology**] it actually *is* possible. I've certainly worked with a number of people who have had this problem, and it has not been at all easy to stop, and yet it is possible. With a lot of hard work it really can be done. It's something I'd love to help you with. [**Validating—Cheerleading**]

C: I don't know.

ROLE PLAY #2: COMMITMENT STRATEGIES

This is a continuation of the first session with Ashley. The therapist demonstrates several commitment strategies as she attempts to solidify Ashley's commitment to eliminating self-harm.

T: I understand that you have tried to kill yourself twice, is that right?

C: M'hmm.

T: That you overdosed on two occasions and that also you're currently harming yourself by cutting your arms, is that right? [**Eliciting the details of suicide attempts and self-harm history**]

C: M'hmm.

T: Is there any other way in which you're harming yourself right now?

C: No, that's it.

T: When did you last actually cut your arms? [**Eliciting specifics of the problem behavior**]

C: This morning.

T: Too bad. [**Genuine, direct expression of therapist disappointment; an aversive contingency**] What did you cut them with, actually?

C: A razor from the bathroom.

T: I guess one of the things I'm wondering is whether or not it's your goal to eliminate the self-harm and suicidal behavior. Like, do you want my help with that? [**Eliciting Commitment**]

C: I don't think you can help with it, I mean, it's been a long time.

T: It's been a long time that you've been doing it. [**Validating—Reflecting**] Well, and I kind of imagine there's probably some function that it's serving, so I'm imagining it's doing something for you. [**Validating in the context of pathology—maladaptive behavior patterns develop for understandable reasons**]

C: M'hmm.

T: So what's the self-harm behavior doing for you? [**Eliciting Pros and Cons (starting with Pros)**]

C: It's just a relief, like, when I'm really anxious or really upset about something, I find it's the only thing that really calms me down.

T: So it really works to take your anxiety down?

C: Yeah.

T: Is it anxiety, and is there more? When you said relief, relief from what?

C: My life.

T: You say that and you have a look of pain. [**Validating—Reflecting**] Is it pain also?

C: It's just a lot of crap.

T: So, in the moment, it sounds like the real issue is that you've got a lot of pain and a lot of anxiety, and when you cut yourself it actually reduces the intensity of those emotions. [**Identifying self-harm as an attempted solution to an underlying painful emotion**]

C: Yeah.

T: So it sounds like that's the *real* problem.

C: I guess.

T: I don't know if it's what you want, but I'm thinking that if you're interested in finding other ways to reduce anxiety and reduce pain, then that's something we could work on. [**Eliciting Commitment**]

C: I don't know if that's possible.

T: My guess is it would be pretty damn hard to do it, [**Validating—Reflecting**] *and*, I have no doubt that if it's what you want, then you can get there, and I would help you do that. [**Commitment strategy— Cheerleading**] [**Dialectical balancing of acceptance and change**] What I *don't* want to do is I don't want to push you to do something that you're not interested in. [**Eliciting Commitment**]

C: I'm interested; I just . . . I don't know.

T: So why? Why would you want to stop self-harming? [**Playing "Devil's Advocate"**]

C: I just want a normal life, be a normal person.

T: I can understand that. [**Validating—Normalizing**] So how is it getting in the way of that? [**Eliciting Pros and Cons: (moving to Cons)**]

C: I feel self-conscious about it. I get so upset all the time, out of control. It makes me feel out of control.

T: I get that. I can imagine why it would make you feel more out of control. [**Validation—Normalizing**] So if I could help you find ways to eliminate the self-harm behavior and suicidal behavior *and* find a way to reduce all the negative emotions that you're currently trying

to reduce . . . would you want my help with that? [**Eliciting commitment with Integration of Pros and Cons**]

C: Yeah, but it's a large order to fill.

T: It is a huge order, and as I said, it's not something you have to do.
You could continue to self-harm and frankly . . . [**Highlighting the
Freedom to Choose**]

C: I don't want to. I want to stop. I don't want to be self-harming.

T: Well, this is good, this is great. [**Positively reinforcing commitment
to change**] If that's what you want, then it really means actually getting rid of all the razors and ruling it out completely. Are you willing
to go all the way? [**Eliciting Commitment**]

C: I want to, but I just don't know if I can.

T: So it sounds like it's kind of, fear is the real issue. You want it and
you're afraid you can't do it. [**Validating—Mind Reading**] It makes
sense, right, because you've been doing it a long time, since age 12?
[**Validating—Making sense in terms of past experience**]

C: M'hmm.

T: It makes sense to be afraid. [**Validating—Making sense in terms of
past experience**]
I'm not so much asking you whether or not you *believe* you can do it
but whether you *want* to get there. [**Clarifying that commitment is
about the desire to make a change**]

C: Yeah, I want to get there.

T: Great. [**Positively reinforcing commitment to change**]

C: Well, how can I do that?

T: I'm so glad you asked—great! [**Positively reinforcing commitment** to change] I mean, because that's something you and I can work on. It's just, if we're going to get you there, then it kind of means turning your mind completely to the idea of not doing it at all. [**Eliciting Commitment**] So we'd have to figure out how you're going to get from this session until our next meeting, to ride through all those painful emotions without self-harming. [**Turning from Commitment to Problem-Solving Strategies**]

ROLE PLAY #3: PROBLEM SOLVING

This is a continuation of the first session with Ashley. The therapist uses several problem-solving strategies to help Ashley eliminate self-harm.

T: I'm so glad that you asked what it is that you can actually do to stop self-harming, so I'm going to jump in and tell you the first thing you've got to do: If you want to stop this behavior, the first thing you've got to do is get rid of whatever you use to self-harm. [**Increasing environmental safety**] You mentioned razors, anything else?

C: No, that's it.

T: So you have got to get rid of those. They've got to be out of the bathroom, out of your house.

C: I don't know.

T: It's scary, isn't it? [**Validation: Mind Reading**]

C: Yeah.

T: I know; it's a really big step. [**Validation: Mind Reading**] I've got to tell you, the reason this is so important, is that if there is something in your environment that is the thing that you typically use to harm yourself with, your brain is going to immediately go to that as a solution. [**Explaining the rationale for increasing environmental safety**]

C: Yeah.

T: And even if you have every good intention of doing something different, your brain is just going to be like, "I know exactly where those are. I'm going there." And it's just going to be so hard to resist that, in fact, probably impossible. We actually know from research that if the means are available, that's going to increase the chance that you'll actually harm yourself. The only way to deal with that is to actually get rid of them.

C: Okay, I'll try.

T: You'll try?

C: Okay, I'll do it.

T: Will you do it? Good for you, that's fantastic. [**Positive reinforcement of commitment**] Will you do that as soon as you get home tonight?

C: Yeah.

T: Awesome. Good for you. So, with that out of the way, this means that you're going to have some pretty intense urges to cope with, so let's actually move into figuring out how to tackle those urges. Are you ready for that? [**Eliciting commitment to the next topic: Problem solving**]

C: Yeah.

T: Okay, fabulous. So when was the last time you harmed yourself? [**Beginning a Behavioral Chain Analysis by defining the problem behavior**] c: This morning.

t: Do you remember what time?

c: Around 11:30.

t: So you cut yourself with razors?

c: Yeah.

t: Can you pinpoint the moment when the urge to cut yourself started? **[Gathering details of the most recent self-harm incident; inquiring about the prompting event]**

c: Just a few minutes before I actually did.

t: What was going on?

c: I got into a fight with my boyfriend on the phone and then when I hung up the phone I, just, really wanted to. **[The prompting event]**

t: So you had a really strong urge when you hung up that phone, okay. So you're telling me there's like 2 minutes . . . you hung up the phone . . . there was 2 minutes when you were just, I'm guessing, overwhelmed with emotion . . . **[Identifying the real problem (overwhelming emotional pain); also Mind Reading]**

c: Yeah.

t: . . . and then you went for the blades at that point. So that's our 2-minute window, to really try to figure out how to work with that really intense emotion and help you get through that crisis—help you get through that crisis without making things worse . . . **[Rationale for distress tolerance skills]**

c: Yeah.

t: That's the key here. So did you try anything? I know it was only 2 minutes—did you try anything to see if you could find another way out of this besides cutting? [**Inquiring about the client's current ways of coping**]

c: Yeah, I walked around my house for a while, for 2 minutes, just trying to calm down.

t: Good for you, so you tried one thing. [**Positively reinforcing the client's attempt to not act on the urge**] And how did that go?

c: It didn't work.

t: Right, okay. Did it work even a little? Did it get your mind off it for a second or get the intensity down at all?

c: Maybe a tiny bit, but not enough.

t: So that's something we could certainly talk about building on, because, for a lot of people, a lot of really intense sensations are the thing that can help them get through that crisis. [**Introducing distress tolerance skills**] Do you do any running, or . . . are you a runner? [**Distress tolerance skills teaching—Asking about intense exercise**]

c: No.

t: Do you like going for walks?

c: Sure.

t: So certainly one option in that moment would be, just, get out of the house.

c: Yeah.

t: Get out, go for a walk. That's not necessarily so intense. Sometimes really hard exercise is one option; that's why I was asking about the running. Some people have even told me they'll do jumping jacks in a moment like that, do 100 jumping jacks right then.

c: Maybe.

T: It may sound weird, but really getting your heart rate up and getting involved in something intense is one way of getting through a really, really difficult moment. Another option would be using the sensation of cold. [**Distress tolerance skills teaching—Using cold temperature**] Have you ever heard of that?

C: No.

T: This is actually effective for a lot of people. There's different ways of doing it. You could go to the freezer, grab an ice cube, hold an ice cube over the sink and just watch it melt. What do you think of that?

C: It doesn't seem . . . it seems weird.

T: Yeah, a lot of people do have that reaction at first. [**Validating: Normalizing**] I hope you try it out, though, because it's actually something that can be quite absorbing. It can really grab your attention. You just keep holding it and squeezing it, no matter how cold it is. For some people, that's pretty distracting. So that's another option. And then just jumping into an ice-cold shower is also a possibility.

C: I guess.

T: I know people who this has really, really worked for. It can be incredibly intense and successful, and there's actually some scientific rationale for that, because it seems like very intense cold brings down your blood pressure and your heart rate, and actually physically slows down that massively agitated state.

C: Okay.

T: So those are some ideas to help you get through when you've got some really intense urges.

C: Okay, I guess I'll try it.

T: Terrific, so, good for you. I'm glad you're up for those ideas. [**Positive reinforcement of willingness to try new strategies**] Now I also just wanted to check in . . . When you go home after our meeting today, you've made a wonderful commitment to throw away your blades. What do you think might get in the way of actually doing that? [**Troubleshooting commitment to increase environmental safety**]

C: That I just don't want to.

T: I could totally understand that. You've mentioned that it's been a part of your life and something that you've been attached to. [**Validating: Normalizing in the context of past experience**] So you think maybe you could go home and change your mind?

C: Yeah, totally.

T: So how can we problem solve around that one? What would keep your resolve up? Can you think of anything you could tell yourself when you get home, to just really remember how important this is?

C: That I just don't want to be doing it anymore.

T: Fantastic. [**Positively reinforcing the client's suggestion**] Do you think that's enough? Is that strong enough to help you stay on target? [**Continuing troubleshooting**]

C: I guess I can try it and see.

T: So trying it and see is one thing. Another thing is, how are you going to remember that you're going to tell yourself that? Do you need to write it down? [**Offering a troubleshooting suggestion**]

C: Maybe write it down.

T: Okay, maybe in a minute we can write that down. So that's one idea. What else? [**Continuing troubleshooting**] We should go back to when you were telling me about the reasons that you actually don't want to self-harm anymore. So remembering that you don't want to is great, and what are the actual reasons? Remind us of those. **[Strengthening Commitment—Review Pros and Cons]**

c: I just want to be in control of things.

t: Fantastic. **[Positively reinforcing her recollection and participation in the discussion]**

c: I want to look like a normal person.

t: Great. No more Band-aids, no more scars.

c: Yeah.

t: Excellent. So if you wrote that all out and had this list in front of you when you went home, do you think that would help you remember? And help you stay committed to actually doing it?

c: Yeah.

t: Alright. One more thought that I have is, if you do those things and you find that you're still not that sure and having trouble doing it, would you call me? **[Continuing troubleshooting—offering some between-session contact to increase the likelihood of following through on a very difficult plan]**

c: Yes.

t: So I'm going to be here until 5:00, so if you get home and you lose your commitment around that, you give me a call and I will try to help you get it back.

c: Okay, thanks.

t: Excellent.

ROLE PLAY #4: AVIS-R SKILLS COACHING PROTOCOL

Two weeks later, Ashley enters a session in an emotionally dysregulated state. The therapist coaches her to use skills to regulate her emotions. Then they begin a Behavioral Chain Analysis.

C: I'm so angry. I'm so angry at that jerk. You know what? I'm going to quit my job. I'm going to quit because he just . . . it's not even my fault that that thing happened. It's not even my fault that those guys were fighting. I wasn't even serving them. You know what, I'm sick of it.

T: Ashley, one sec. Take a minute. [**Attending to the client—Assess the problem behavior**]

C: I'm going to quit. I'm just . . .

T: Ashley, I don't know what's happening but it looks pretty intense. [**Validating the client's emotional pain**]

C: Yeah, it's intense.

T: You look really uncomfortable. [**Validating: Reflecting**]

C: I'm so uncomfortable and I'm so . . . I'm just angry at that guy. He's just a jerk. I don't know why it's my fault.

T: Okay, so it sounds like a lot has happened, something happened at work and it looks pretty intense right now. [**Validating: Reflecting**]

C: Yeah. I'm going to quit. Can I quit? Is that okay?

T: Hey, you know what, my guess is right now it's going to be really hard to problem solve this when you're feeling this way. [**Starting to offer a rationale for helping her with her feelings before deciding what to do about the job**]

C: Yeah, but you know what, I don't know if I can do anything except be upset right now, okay, and I don't understand . . .

T: I understand that it's hard to think clearly [**Validating: Reflecting**] and I'm wondering right now, do you want . . . because it looks like you're . . . I don't know if it's fear, or anger or what. [**Identifying Emotion**]

C: No, I'm just, I'm mad.

T: Yeah, it looks it. [**Validating: Reflecting**] Do you want some help to try to get yourself more regulated so you can figure out a way to solve whatever has happened here? [**Inviting the client to use a skill and give a rationale**]

C: Yeah, sure, fine, whatever.

T: I know it's hard. I appreciate you trying to work on this right now, given how damn hard it must be. [**Validating the difficulty of trying to use a skill**]

C: Really, I'm just so angry and I so can't take the job anymore. I just don't know why I'm doing it in the first place.

T: Okay, so something happened at work today.

C: Yes.

T: And it looks really hard [**Validating the client's pain**], and it sounds like we should try to sort this out and we've got to figure this one out . . .

C: I don't know what to figure out.

T: You what?

C: There's just nothing to figure out; that's all there is to it.

T: And my guess is, right now, given how . . . and, good, you're breathing right now because I think that's one of the ways to get yourself more regulated, [**Positively reinforcing the client's efforts to self-regulate**] because it looks like something big has happened and if we're

going to help you sort it out, somehow we've got to help you stay more
regulated here, okay? [**Repeating the invitation**]

c: Fine.

t: What about trying some deep breathing? Want to try that together?
[**50:18 Instructing the client on how to use the skill**]

c: Okay.

t: Good for you [**Positive reinforcement of agreement to try a skill**],
I know it's hard. [**Validating difficulty**] I like the fact that you put
your feet on the ground right now, because that might help ground
you [**Positively reinforcing her efforts**], but just right now bring
your attention to your breath, we can do this together, really deep
breaths. [**Showing the skill and seeing the client use the skill**]

Okay, great, this is great. Keep breathing; just take deep breaths. We
will get you through this. [**Cheerleading**] Just right now bring your
full attention to your breath. Maybe take a couple more really deep
breaths. Okay, fabulous, this is great. [**Reinforcing adaptive behavior**] Let me ask you right now, how dysregulated are you feeling on
a scale of 0 to 10? How intense is it? [**Reviewing the helpfulness of
the new skill**]

c: Maybe 6.

t: Compared to how you were when you just came in, has it come
down, been the same, or gone up?

c: Come down.

t: Okay, fabulous, good for you. So, here's the thing, my guess is when
we start talking about whatever happened at work today, probably,
you might find that your emotions get more intense again, and I think

what we need to do is just bring your attention back to your breath if that happens, so we can find a way to help you get more regulated. [**Orienting the client to the likelihood that emotional pain will return and skill will need to be practiced again**] Because I think that if we can help you stay regulated, then we can problem solve whatever has gone on. [**Reminder of a rationale for staying regulated**]

c: Okay.

t: Okay, great, I appreciate your willingness. [**Positively reinforcing her engagement**] I know it's hard to do when you're feeling really upset. [**Validating the difficulty**] I don't exactly know what's happened today at work but it sounds like something major went down . . . [**Begin the Behavioral Chain Analysis with the client's description of the event and her emotions**]

c: Yeah. I'm going to quit, because I can't . . .

t: So you want to quit right now. [**Validating: Reflecting**] Have you quit, by the way, already?

c: No, I just walked out.

t: Fabulous that you didn't quit. Okay, this is great. [**Positively reinforcing adaptive behavior**] My guess is, if you're feeling this emotional, it's going to be hard to think clearly and figure out what makes sense. . . . [**Explaining why it's great that she did not walk out—she didn't act on the intense emotion which may impair her decision making**]

c: Yeah, but you know what, I just don't want to think about it anymore, and it causes me more stress than it's worth, you know what I mean?

t: Okay, yeah.

c: If I just didn't have to do it, then I wouldn't . . . you know what I mean, I just wouldn't have to worry about it.

t: Okay, I can see right now, I notice even as you're talking, do you notice you're looking more anxious and more dysregulated again? [Validating: Attending to an in-session emotion] Just take some deep breaths. [Reminder of the skill] We will sort this out; we will help you find a way through this. That I have no doubt we can do, okay? [Cheerleading]

c: M'hmm.

t: So just keep bringing yourself back to your breath when you notice yourself getting really undone. [Attending to in-session emotions and returning to skills coaching (breathing)] So why don't we wind it back to what set things off today that got you thinking of quitting work, [Identifying the prompting event] because I don't exactly know what happened.

c: I went in like any other shift, whatever, and then about halfway through there were these two guys sitting at the bar and they were being kind of obnoxious but they weren't my table, I wasn't serving them. And then by the end of the night they were totally drunk, and it wasn't my responsibility, it was the bartender who was serving them, and then my boss comes up to me and tells me that it's my fault and that I should be more responsible and that I'm being irresponsible in my job. And, I'm like, I'm not being irresponsible in my job, it wasn't even my table, you know what I mean? And I just think that he's really disrespectful when he talks to me like that.

t: So, wow, it sounds pretty frustrating. It sounds like your boss accused you of . . . [Validating: Reflecting]

C: Totally. Why would he do that to me?

T: Yeah, and I . . .

C: He's a jerk, you know. He's a jerk.

T: My guess is, right now, you having all these judgments of him is probably actually just going to make you angrier. [**Interrupting the Behavioral Chain Analysis to attend to in-session thoughts and emotions; highlighting the connection between judgmental thoughts and anger**]

C: Yeah, it's making me angry because I think that he's a real, you know . . . he wasn't thinking about what he was saying.

T: Okay, that may be true and just right now, if we're going to help you problem solve it, and if we want to help you keep your anger down, it may be helpful just to drop the judgments of him. [**Coaching to take a nonjudgmental stance in order to help her stay regulated**]

C: But you know . . .

T: Do you want to give that a shot? [**Eliciting Commitment**] I know it's hard. [**Validating: Mind Reading**]

C: Fine.

T: Yeah? I mean, you could let yourself go, if you want, judging him and calling him a jerk and that's certainly an option. It's just, I think the more you do it, just the more upset you get and then it becomes impossible for us to problem solve. [**Highlighting the Freedom to Choose in the absence of alternatives**]

C: Okay.

T: Okay?

C: Yeah.

T: I appreciate your willingness. So, wind it back, you're at work and he basically accuses you of serving these guys who are drunk. [**Resume the Behavioral Chain Analysis—clarifying the prompting event**]

C: Yeah, and they weren't even my table. Like, he somehow thought that it was my responsibility.

T: So what did he actually say, by the way? [**Clarifying exactly what the prompting event was, verbatim**]

C: He said, "Ashley, maybe you could keep an eye on things a little bit more."

T: In that tone?

C: Yeah, it was a disgusting tone.

T: Are you noticing your judgments there? [**Highlighting her in-session judgmental thoughts**] So he accuses you of just not taking care of things and I can imagine feeling . . . hurt? [**A link in the chain after the prompting event: The emotion of hurt**]

C: Yeah, I was hurt.

T: Which makes sense. I don't like to be accused of things that I'm not doing. I don't think anybody does. [**Validating: Normalizing**] So how did you get from there to now thinking you're going to quit work? [**Examining the links in the chain; what connects her boss's statement (and the client's hurt) to the urge to quit?**]

C: Well, because then he accused me of that and then I guess I talked back to him and said that it wasn't my fault, and then he said that I should maybe think twice before I talk, and then I said, "I'm out of here."

T: Okay, hold on. When you say you talked back to him, what did you actually say?

C: I said it wasn't my responsibility. They weren't even my table.

T: Did you say it in that tone?

C: I don't know; I was angry.

T: Yeah, okay. It sounds to me like the real issue is you felt pretty hurt by him. [**Identifying the real problem (underlying painful emotion)**]

C: Yeah, especially because I know him because he's my boyfriend's brother, so it's like we kind of have a relationship.

T: Well, I imagine even if you didn't know him . . . I'd feel pretty hurt by somebody accusing me of doing something that I'm not doing. [**Validating: Normalizing**]

C: Yeah.

T: So that makes sense. The piece I'm trying to figure out is, how do you get from . . . because you said you felt real hurt and then you said some things to him. [**Further examining links between the prompting event and problem behavior**] When you said you kind of mouthed off at him, what does that mean exactly? [**Clarifying the links**]

C: Well, I just told him it wasn't my responsibility and that he should not speak to people the way he does, and I just said that I thought he was kind of being a jerk.

T: Oh, did you say that?

C: Yeah, but he, but I . . .

T: Too bad, okay. [**Being direct and genuine and providing an aversive contingency: The therapist expresses disappointment in maladaptive behavior**] So it sounds like you were understandably upset and hurt [**Validating: Normalizing**] and it sounds like you kind of lost it with him. [**Being genuine and direct while confronting a client with maladaptive behavior**]

c: Yeah.

t: Okay, too bad. So, look, I think it makes sense that you said something to him. [**Validating: Normalizing**] Probably calling him a jerk wasn't the most effective thing. [**Genuine, direct confrontation, without judgment**]

c: Yeah, but I was . . . whatever.

t: Am I sounding like I'm attacking when I say that right now?

c: Well, yeah, it just feels like . . . I was upset and maybe that was stupid but . . .

t: Yeah, I've got to tell you right now, my intent is not to attack you or put you down [**Clarifying intention**]. I do get that if you weren't doing something that you're being accused of doing, you'd be really hurt and probably a bit angry. [**Validating: Normalizing**]

c: Yeah.

t: I think that's normal, and I think it makes perfect sense that you tried to talk to him. [**Validating: Normalizing**] I'm kind of thinking, probably calling him a jerk wasn't necessarily the most helpful thing. [**Genuine, direct confrontation, without judgment**] Do you agree?

c: Yeah.

t: Okay. It sounds like the real issue, that maybe we could work on, is how to communicate to him really directly in an effective way. [**Interweaving Solution Analysis into Behavioral Analysis—an ineffective link to work on is calling the boss a jerk; need to help her find other ways to express hurt and justified anger**]

C: M'hmm.

T: But let's shelve that for a moment because I'm still trying to figure out, how do you get from there to thinking of quitting? Because that's the piece I'm still not quite sure about. [**Eliciting more links between the prompting event and the problem behavior**]

C: So I left and when I got home I thought, it's too much, and I didn't want to go back there and face him, because now he's angry at me and I'm angry at him, and maybe I just don't need the job. Maybe I could find something else or just not work.

T: So it sounds like . . . I don't know if it's shame, shame at going back to him, and also anger? [**Identifying another underlying painful emotion; Mind Reading that the link that led to the urge to quit was the emotion of shame**]

C: Yeah, I think both. Well, I don't know. I guess. I feel bad but I'm still upset with him even though I feel bad.

T: Yeah, you're still angry with him. [**Validating: Reflecting**] So would you want my help figuring out how to approach him and communicate to him in an effective way? [**Beginning a Solution Analysis by eliciting commitment to work on interpersonal skills (expression of hurt)**]

C: Yeah, because I'm sick of this kind of thing happening.

T: Yeah, I can understand that. [**Validating: Normalizing**] I know this job has been important to you and I can't imagine right now that quitting is going to be so helpful. [**Rationale for working on speaking to the boss directly rather than quitting**]

C: Maybe you're right.

T: So why don't we work on figuring out how you can approach him and talk about what happened . . .

C: Okay. [**Agreement reached to work on interpersonal effectiveness as a solution to the real problem**]

T: . . . because it sounds pretty important. Okay?

C: M'hmm.

They proceed to discuss how Ashley can approach her boss in an effective way.

Once the dysfunctional links surrounding the problematic behaviors have been identified, they can be repaired in numerous ways. These may include skills training in interpersonal effectiveness, such as helping clients to communicate their emotions and needs more directly without hostility.

C: So it's been 6 months since I started coming here and I think now I have a little bit more of an understanding about how my anxiety fueled my self-harm, so although I'm a bit nervous to say that out loud, I feel like I have a bit more control over things. I've been working at the bar a bit more often, which feels good, I guess, and I haven't cut for 3 months and I feel kind of confident in wearing shorter sleeves and not being so self-conscious about it. And, yeah, I'm feeling like I'm getting somewhere.

Appendix B:
Practice Reminder Summary

(Refer to the enclosed Practice Reminder Card.)

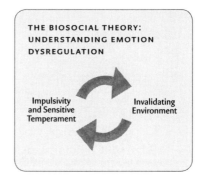

Stay Compassionate

(1) Use the biosocial theory: "Based on
the interaction between this individual's temperament and caregivers, he
or she simply couldn't have turned out any other way."

(2) Hold helpful assumptions about clients:
- They are doing the best they can.
- They want to improve.
- They need to do better, try harder, and be more motivated to change.
- They may not have caused all of their own problems, but they have to solve them.

- The lives of suicidal emotionally dysregulated clients are unbearable.
- They must learn new behaviors in all relevant contexts.
- It is not a client's fault if she or he does not change.
- Therapists working with difficult clients need support.

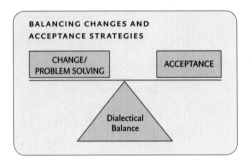

Be Validating: Communicate that something about the client's behavior makes sense or is **understandable** within the current context by:

- listening with full attention, without bias or judgment;
- paraphrasing and reflecting;
- verbalizing unarticulated thoughts, feelings, and urges (i.e., suffering and pain, difficulty with a task); be willing to be corrected;
- making **sense** of your client's behaviors, urges, thoughts, and feelings, based on their past learning, their thinking, or their biology;
- **normalizing** your client's behaviors, urges, thoughts, and feelings, in terms of what is true for most; and
- being **radically genuine,** treating your client as an individual who is capable, competent, effective, and reasonable—not fragile.

Use Commitment Strategies:

- **Elicit** a clear commitment for any plan: "Are you willing to . . . ?"
- Explore the **Pros and Cons** of the behavior and of changing; clarify why it makes sense that the person has developed this habit and what he or she will be giving up if change happens.
- Play the **Devil's Advocate**: Argue against changing (e.g., by emphasizing the cons of changing) to increase the intensity of commitment and prepare for future doubts: "Why *would* you want to change?"
- **Foot-in-the-Door and Door-in-the-Face**: Request a commitment to change something extremely challenging and then revise, if needed, to something more realistic.
- **Connect to Prior Commitments**
- **Highlight the Freedom to Choose and the Absence of Alternatives**: "You have the freedom to choose that, and, it won't help you meet your goals."
- **Generate Hope** or Cheerlead.

Problem Solve by (1) identifying the real problem underlying the self-harm or impulsive behaviors, which are usually a means to solve another problem (e.g., emotional pain); (2) increasing environmental safety (manage triggering cues and remove access to what the client uses to self-harm); and (3) using distress tolerance skills.

Distress Tolerance: Coach clients to engage in an intense experience or sensation, shifting their attention away from the painful emotion and/or helping reduce arousal with the use of **cold temperatures** (holding an ice cube or ice pack, ice-cold shower), **intense exercise** (fast walking, jogging, bicycling, jumping jacks) and **mindful breathing;** practice when NOT in distress.

AVIS-R Skills Coaching Protocol for acute, in-session emotional dysregulation:

1. ATTEND to the client and the problem.
2. ASSESS the problem behavior.
3. VALIDATE the pain that led to the problem.
4. VALIDATE the difficulty of trying to change/using skills.
5. INVITE the client to use a skill and give a rationale.
6. INSTRUCT the client on how to use the skill.
7. SHOW or model the skill.
8. SEE the client use the skill.
9. REINFORCE (praise) adaptive behavior.
10. REVIEW and get feedback on the helpfulness of the new skill/ behavior.

Behavioral Chain Analysis

1. Identify the specific behavior: Record the day it occurred, what time, what location, how long it took and how severe it was; overt actions (self-harm, an angry outburst, a binge-eating episode, or an incident of substance use) as well as covert experiences (painful emotions, dysfunctional thoughts, or urges to harmfully act).

2. Identify vulnerabilities: They may be rooted in the distant past (a history of childhood abuse) or in the recent past (an interpersonal conflict, a medication change, or a physical illness).

3. Identify the prompting event: It can be seen as the first link in the chain toward the behavior; it is often interpersonal, although a trigger can also be internal, such as a flashback or a physical sensation. Inquire about what was going on when the client first noticed an urge to engage in the problem behavior.

4. Identify the links that connect the prompting event to the behavior: All emotions, thoughts, urges, and actions that occurred between the prompting event and the behavior are of interest. Productive or healthy responses need to be strengthened, and problematic ones need to be altered. Carefully examine the client's decision-making process. Try to isolate the moment when the client made the decision to engage in the behavior (e.g., he or she may have had the thought "I refuse to tolerate this pain any longer")—this will allow him or her to develop greater understanding and control over impulsive behaviors that can seem to happen out of the blue.

5. Identify the consequences: Inadvertent reinforcers may include increased attention (positive or negative) from important people in the client's life, such as the whole family meeting him or her in the emergency room—even if the family members are angry.

Appendix C: Answer Key

LESSON PLAN #1

A. Discussion

There are many right answers. These are just examples.

1. <u>Description</u>: I feel frustrated when my client calls me several times weekly in tears and says, "I have no idea what skill to use," even though we have been reviewing skills every week lately.
    <u>Why this makes perfect sense</u>: I think her frequent calling in a helpless state is perfectly understandable because she was a very sensitive, emotional child who was taunted by her older brother, bullied at school, and consistently neglected by her mother. When her mother did pay attention to her, it was to roll her eyes at how sensitive my client was and to make sarcastic remarks

about the fact that she was crying *again*. How could she *not* have developed into someone who gets desperate for soothing attention when she is distressed? And how could she possibly think clearly when she is crying, if she expects that people will be irritated and dismissive? She just couldn't be otherwise.

2. Validating statements.

   a. "What's the point?" *You must be feeling so frustrated and discouraged.* (mind read—name the emotion) *You've wanted to change this for so long and it just hasn't happened yet.* (makes sense in context of history) [Later, you might talk about what the point actually is, but remember to validate first.]

   b. [after you have been late for the last two meetings:] "It's obvious you don't care about me—you've been late for our last two meetings." *I understand you're feeling really disrespected by that.* (reflect/mind read—name the emotional experience) *I too might get the message someone didn't care if he kept coming late.* (normalize) [Then, go on to apologize and explain (if it is true) that your lateness was not because of not caring, and (presuming this is also true) that you are fixing the situation so you will come on time in the future. Or that you would like to change the appointment time to one that is more doable for you.]

   c. [when you have *not* actually been late for the last two meetings, although you have been in the past:] "It's obvious you don't care about me—you've been late for our last two meetings." *My goodness, I can certainly imagine being hurt* (mind read—name the emotion; normalize) *if you're thinking I've been late for the past two meetings.* (make sense in the context of an incorrect thought) *You know, I've been keeping track of my timeliness and I am sure I was on time the past few weeks. Now, I know I wasn't always on time a few weeks ago, so I would certainly understand if that memory was still fresh in your mind, since I recognize it really bothered you a lot.* (make sense in the context of how memory commonly works) [Then explore why the client thought you were late.]

d. "You're not helping me at all." *You are really feeling frustrated with me.* (mind read—name the emotion)

e. "I wish I wasn't so out of control. I'm such a loser." *Hmm, you get really ashamed and angry with yourself when you act out of control.* (mind read—name the emotions) *Also I bet you feel even worse when you call yourself names—I know I do.* (normalize) [Rather than reassure that she is not a loser, suggest noticing that that is a judgment and letting go of the thought, just nonjudgmentally describing what the behavior was, and then working on it together without name calling.]

f. "Self-harm is the only thing that helps me in my life; without it I would be dead." *You've always been really clear with me about how well self-harm works to numb your painful emotions. I know you see it as something that gets rids of the medium-severe emotions before they get out of control and you get suicidal. I get how it seems protective.*

(reflect / mind read) However, self-harm doesn't actually work that way: By preventing you from actually learning to cope with your painful emotions, it is keeping you at risk for suicide. Plus, we know that people who self-harm are at MUCH higher risk for suicide than people who don't, including by accident, even if you aren't even trying to kill yourself. So I have to tell you, I get where you're coming from AND self-harm is not protecting you from killing yourself. (not validating what isn't valid)

LESSON PLAN #2

A. Discussion

1. The answers are in the transcription.
2. The answers are in the transcription.
3. <u>Devil's Advocate</u>: "I see what you're saying. It's true, anything could happen. After all, we can't control fate. So . . . why bother with treatment then?"

   <u>Freedom to Choose</u>: "You can choose to kill yourself if you want to and I can't stop you. However, if you do I won't be able to continue to work with you, which would be very disappointing." OR "We will not be able to continue working toward getting better housing." An alternative: "Listen, you are free to choose your path, and I gotta tell ya, if you work on trying to kill yourself while I'm working on trying to improve your life, we will not get anywhere and we'll both

end up really frustrated in our relationship. So in order for me to accept you into this service, I need to know that you and I are on the same page. Are we both working on improving your life? (if yes) Great! So that means you are ruling out suicide?"

<u>Foot-in-the-Door/Door-in-the-Face</u>: If the client says anxiously, "A year! That's like forever, I don't know if I can make that commitment!" Therapist: "Well, how long *will* you make a commitment for?" Then negotiate a period of time and remember to raise it again at that time for a recommitment.

B. Experiential Tasks

1. <u>Pros and Cons</u>: "Oh!" (trying to contain your incredulity) "Tell me about how that will work." (elicit pros) "I see, well, and I guess it's simple and cheap too!" (continue with pros) "Have you thought about any downsides?" (wonder about cons) "Do you worry you might get hungry?" (see if you can elicit other cons; if not, gradually suggest more but continue to validate the pros) "Weak? Unable to think? Dead?"

    <u>Freedom to Choose</u>: "I mean, look, you can do that, I just gotta tell ya, I'm not sure what the point of dieting is if it kills you."

    <u>Devil's Advocate</u>: "Well, I see where you're coming from." (list the pros you have already discussed) "I mean, I guess it can't go wrong, hey? There's absolutely no way you could maintain the weight you're at, if you eat nothing. Seems

kind of foolproof! Is there any way I can help you with it? Make sure you work straight through the lunch hour so you don't think about eating? Remind you not to put sugar or cream in your coffee? In fact—are you sure you want to drink anything for the month? I mean, maybe it'll be easier to stop eating if you just don't put anything in your mouth at all. Think about it!" (keep extending his idea until he starts to look doubtful—if never, return to a Freedom to Choose reply like "Seriously, I do think this is crazy. I mean, if this is really what you choose I can't stop you, but I sincerely hope you change your mind.")

2. Very cold temperatures around the eyes lead to a drop in heart rate and blood pressure. This can be calming or relaxing, or, in times of extreme agitation, can actually provide a few moments of emotional relief. It does not tend to have a lasting effect but can help one think clearly for long enough to figure out what other skills to try.

LESSON PLAN #3

A. Discussion

Again, there are many right answers.

1. Stop and engage with her. [Attend] She has already told you what happened so you don't need to assess further now, although later you will want to check for any self-harm urges. "How dreadful!" [Validate] "Listen, I know right now is a super-hard moment to

work on skills, [Validate the difficulty] but I'd love to help you get your breathing under control so you don't pass out!" [Invite] She is looking faint so you get her seated but she is hyperventilating a lot. A colleague brings you two ice packs from the freezer. "Here Jane, hold these." [Instruct] "Put them against your head like this, okay?" You demonstrate or put them against her temples or forehead for her, if you think she is comfortable with that. [Show] "That's it. Just hold them there for a bit, okay? Will you work on breathing with me too? Let's breathe deeply together, all right?" If she nods, continue. "Just breathe into your abdomen, that's it. A few more breaths. Can you feel the cold on your face?" [See] As she settles: "Well done, great job." [Reinforce] "How are you feeling?" [Review] If she is able to breathe and talk, take a few minutes to ensure she is not at risk of suicide or self-harm, then make a skillful plan for getting through the rest of the day.

2. Behavioral Chain Analysis from the Problem-Solving Role Play:

    a. Vulnerabilities: Not covered—need information about whether she was more vulnerable based on lack of sleep, poor eating, other stress, and so on.

    b. Prompting Event: The fight with a boyfriend on the phone—need information about what he said.

    c. Links: Hung up . . . overwhelmed . . . strong urge to self-harm . . . walked around for 2 minutes trying to calm down . . . tiny reduction of agitation—need to know what thoughts she had upon hanging up the phone and how she came to decide to self-harm (e.g. "He hates me, I'm an idiot, we're breaking up, I'll never have another relationship, I'll be alone forever, I can't cope with this, the only way out of this pain is self-harm," etc.).

    d. Problem Behavior: 11:30 am this morning, cut arm with razor—need to know how many, how deeply, whether medical attention was required.

    e. Consequences: not covered—need information about how she felt afterward (relieved and guilty/ashamed, just relieved, upset about the scar) and about whether she told her boyfriend (did he provide soothing and support, which might reinforce self-harming).

B. **Experiential Tasks**

    1. An example: "Sally, I'm so glad you asked for help with this." [Attending to her request, starting with positive reinforcement] "My first question for you is: Do you have alcohol at your place? 'Cause I gotta tell ya, I'm not sure there's any way to avoid drinking if you've got alcohol readily available." [Here, assess her environment and remove cues/means] "It is TOTALLY hard to really throw yourself in and make a full commitment to not coping by drinking!" [Validate the difficulty] "I know what a state you can get into when you ruminate about how incredibly frustrating your boyfriend has been. It's awful." [Validate the pain] "I really want to help you figure out how to cope with your anger without drinking." [Invite] "The hard part is, I think the single biggest factor will be getting rid of any alcohol in your environment." [Instruct] "Otherwise, what's to stop you when you're in that enraged state? What do you think? Are you willing

to get rid of it?" [Invite again. You may not be able to show and see, although you could offer that she could phone you for coaching if she waffles once she gets home. Then you might hear the sound of wine going down the drain.] If she commits: "Wow, I'm so impressed with your willingness. This is really fantastic. And this is SO difficult!" [Reinforcement] "Now, what might get in the way of following through?" [The review might include troubleshooting what part of the plan might go wrong.]

The AVIS-R protocol could be used all over again to coach her to distract or soothe herself in response to the anger she foresees. Reinforcement could also happen between sessions—she could phone to report on her success.

LESSON PLAN #4

Samples are provided below. There are many ways to role play the suggested situations.

A. Discussion

I.   "Lucy, let's look at your early life and think about why it might make perfect sense that you have trouble controlling your emotions. You have described your mother as someone who was impulsive and wasn't so good at controlling her emotions herself, and you've told me you've always had particularly intense emotional reactions for as long as you can remember.

So it seems you probably have what is called an 'emotionally sensitive temperament,' which means you are biologically prone to have such intense emotions that they can be really hard to control. People who have this temperament often need special help learning how to regulate their emotions, but it seems that, instead, your emotions got kind of dismissed by your mother, and she didn't help you figure out what to do with them. On top of that you grew up in a pretty chaotic environment where it was really tough to get to school regularly. In fact it seems you learned that when things aren't just right, staying home from school is what you do. So to me it seems only logical that as an adult you would have trouble regulating your emotions and that it would be particularly hard to get yourself to school regularly."

2. Six ways of validating:

- Fully attend: Listen attentively.
- Paraphrase: "So she was really hitting on him—and right in front of you!"
- Mind read: "Sounds like you felt completely betrayed!" "You just sound SO shocked and angry!"
- Make sense in the context of history: "I can only imagine how hurt you must be, especially given this just happened last month with your other friend!
- Normalizing: "I totally understand your urge to avoid her. When you feel so let down by someone, it's hard to imagine continuing a relationship with them."

- Be radically genuine: "This is such a frustrating situation! And, what I know is, you will figure this one out. You will make your own best decision about how to handle it—I don't know, maybe you do want to stop being friends with her, or maybe you want to talk it over with her and express your feelings, or maybe you want to have a few words with your boyfriend too. If you want any help with any of those ideas, let me know, 'cause I'm sure you and I can figure out a very skilful plan and you will sort this out in a way that works for you."

3.

   a. "Oh, how exciting! Surprise parties are so much fun—and you are so close with your friend—of course you are getting completely swept away with the planning! I'm also thinking it makes perfect sense that you'd be planning to do this instead of going to class, since this is your pattern: something more interesting or engaging comes up, and that immediately takes precedence over the more boring, long-term goals."

   b.

      i. Devil's Advocate: "Hey, why take just one day? Give her a birthday week!" "Why would you want to go to class? This sounds way more engaging!"

      ii. Freedom to Choose and the Absence of Alternatives: "Look, it's entirely your choice whether you go to class or not, and, notice how this is exactly the problem to be solved here in therapy. This is it: Something exciting comes up, and school gets ditched. What you hired me for is to help you in exactly this situation: to figure out how you can still get to class even in the face of strong emotions. Now, you don't have to do it, yet here we are with exactly the opportunity we need in order to help you meet your goal."

    iii. Pros and Cons: "Let's take a minute to review the pros and cons here. What do you think is the upside to spending your day on the party? [pause and discuss] What's the downside to missing class?"

    iv. Connecting to Prior Commitments: "You swore up and down that your goal was to get this program finished so you could be a lab tech. In fact you completely convinced me! Are you changing your goals on me now?"

B. Experiential Tasks

  I. a.

    i. "You've mentioned that you cut yourself when you get overwhelmed by different emotions. It seems to me the real problem here is that when that intense emotional pain happens, you are completely at a loss and just don't know what to do about it. You are looking for some way out and you've discovered that harming yourself brings relief. But that doesn't really solve the problem—the emotions keep coming back, as intense as ever. Your challenge is to find some way, not just of getting relief or escaping from those painful emotions, but to figure out how to actually experience them—without avoiding them—so that over time they can get less overwhelming."

ii. Questions could include: "What have you been using to cut yourself with?" [if something specific:] "Will you get rid of it? Keep in mind that if you see it or know it's there, you'll be likely to turn to it in an overwhelmed moment." Even if he has been using kitchen knives, you could encourage him to get rid of them, or hide them (e.g., put them in a bag and cover it with several layers of packing tape), and eat only food that can be cut with butter knives for a few weeks, while he breaks the self-harm habit.

iii. Practice negotiating with him about which skills might be helpful when he is overwhelmed. Review using cold temperature, intense exercise, deep breathing, or anything else that might be distracting in such a moment.

b. "Dave! Dave, what's happened?" [He chokes out a brief explanation of the phone call.] Wow, you are SO overwhelmed. It sounds like that self-hatred is really rearing its ugly head right now—how painful! Listen, it can be really hard to try something new when you're in the midst of this much pain. Would you like some help right now in figuring out how to tolerate your emotions?" [assuming he says yes] "Fantastic—let's try focusing on our breath right now, okay? Just bring your full attention to your breathing, put your hand on your abdomen to feel your diaphragm expanding [demonstrate, take a deep breath, observe him doing the same thing], that's it, great. Let's do it again." [after a few breaths, assuming he has stopped hyperventilating] "Well done, Dave. How are you feeling now?"

c. Behavioral Chain Analysis: "Let's really analyze this incident of self-harm, and see if we can understand all the factors that led up to it, and that are maintaining this behavior." [pause to ensure he is on board, if not, use commitment strategies] Start by reviewing the problem behavior: when it happened, what he used, how long it took, and so on. Ask about the prompting event: "What do you think set it off, or started you on the path to self-harming? What was the trigger, or prompting event?" Ask about vulnerabilities: "Do you think there were things going on in the background that made you more vulnerable to getting overwhelmed by that call?" Ask about links: "Let's review all the steps (thoughts, emotions, urges, actions) that happened between getting that call and harming yourself." [when he describes going to the movie:] "That's great, I'm so glad you were deliberately trying to figure out a way to tolerate this and to stop ruminating! Too bad it backfired though!" Ask about consequences: "And what happened after? How did you feel? Were there any effects on or reactions from other people?"

Here is a possible summary of the behavioral chain analysis components (depending on what he tells you):

- Vulnerabilities: Poor night's sleep; tendency to ruminate; judgments about the lawyer and about himself
- Prompting Event: Last meeting with the lawyer 2 days beforehand
- Links (use your imagination): (Some ideas:) Ever since the meeting, he has been plaguing himself with the thought that the lawyer hates him and is trying to "screw him over," and he has been ruminating about all the other injustices that have occurred in his life. The night before he harmed himself, he noticed he was getting more and more miserable from dwelling on it and went out to a movie to distract himself. However, the movie was about a divorcing couple and he felt even more agitated afterward and then couldn't sleep. He had nightmares about losing his store and his house. He woke up early in a cold sweat, feeling hopeless and like he just "can't take it any longer." He began thinking about the relief he would get from cutting himself and thought, "Screw it—I don't care if my goal in therapy is to regulate my emotions; this is more than one person can take." When it occurred to him to undo the razor, he felt excited and giddy.
- Problem Behavior: As described above
- Consequences: He felt a bit high, a sort of "delicious, floaty relief" after scraping his arm. He also had a "triumphant" feeling that he now has proof of how much damage his ex-wife and the lawyer have done to him. After about 15 minutes he began to worry about whether he would be permanently disfigured from the scrape and

wondered if he should go to the doctor. He decided not to, because he was too ashamed that he had done this to himself. He then judged himself as an "idiot, a weakling, and a loser" and realized that he felt no better than he had the night before. He also felt ashamed about letting you down; otherwise, he has told no one and has kept it hidden.

- Brainstorming: "It seems like we need to do some more work on your ruminating. I'm so glad you noticed it and tried distracting. What other solutions can you think of?" You may raise any number of ideas: having a long list of potential distractions (and being careful not to choose things that are thematically related to his worries); working on taking a nonjudgmental stance toward himself; thought stopping; setting aside 20 to 30 minutes daily to worry/ruminate and not allowing himself to do so at any other time, and so on.

"Let's have a look at those links between the prompting event and the actual self-harm. Which ones do you think we can work on strengthening, and which ones should we try changing?" Reinforce his awareness that he was ruminating and his decision to try distracting. Encourage him not to give up even if one distracting attempt backfires—what else could he have done after the movie? (Could he have left the movie early?) What other skills could he use when he is feeling agitated? (Cold water or ice, exercise, breathing, other distractions, etc.). Could he use commitment strategies with himself when he starts to say, "Why bother; there's no point?" For example, he could review the pros and cons of self-harm; connect to his commitment by remembering that he made this a goal for some important reasons. What about having some emergency hope-generating statements taped to the wall or mirror?

QUIZ

1. What are the three features of an emotionally sensitive temperament?

   - More sensitive to stimuli/quicker to respond
   - More intense responses
   - Emotions last longer/slower return to baseline

2. What are the three theories or philosophies that form the theoretical basis of DBT?

   - Learning Theory
   - Zen philosophy
   - Dialectical philosophy

3. a. "Clearly this is painful to talk about, and it's really important! Let's sort out what needs to happen so you are for sure here on time next week."

4. b. Mind reading

5. c. Validating based on history
6. e. Cheerleading
7. c. Validating based on history
8. a. Devil's Advocate
9. d. Highlight the Freedom to Choose
10. c. Connect to Prior Commitments
11. e. Generate Hope
12. b. "Mary, this is dreadful! How could you not be completely overwhelmed!? Here's an ice pack—hold on to that now and bring your full attention to it."
13. c. Having impulsive sex
14. d. Fighting with his parents
15. b. Drinking alcohol in the afternoon
16. a. C, D, E, and F
17. d. H and I
18. d. He has difficulty regulating anger and anxiety.
19. d. He is exploitative and manipulative.
20. a. Validation
21. d. Skills coaching
22. b. Commitment
23. e. None of the above
24. c. Problem solving
25. b. "You're really discouraged about the prospect of changing this. You've tried before and it just seemed too hard."
26. d. "So why *would* you want to work on this problem with me?"
27. e. She has not made a commitment to work on this behavior.

References

Bohus, M., Haaf, B., Sims, T., Limberger, M. F., Schmahl, C., Unckel, C., et al. (2004). Evaluation of inpatient dialectical-behavioral therapy for borderline personality disorder: A controlled trial. *Behaviour Research and Thearpy, 42,* 487–499.

Carter, G. L., Wilcox, C. H., Lewin, T. J., Conrad, A. M., & Bendit, N. (2010). Hunter DBT project: A randomized controlled trial of dialectical behaviour therapy in women with borderline personality disorder. *Australian and New Zealand Journal of Psychiatry, 44,* 162–173.

Clarkin, J. F., Levy, K. N., Lenzenweger, M. F., & Kernberg, O. F. (2007). Evaluating three treatments for borderline personality disorder: A multiwave study. *American Journal of Psychiatry, 164*(6), 922–928.

Crowell, S. E., Beauchaine, T. P., & Linehan, M. M. (2009). A biosocial developmental model of borderline personality: Elaborating and extending Linehan's theory. *Psychological Bulletin, 135*(3), 495–510.

Dimeff, L. A., & Koerner, K. (Eds.). (2007). *Dialectical behavior therapy in clinical practice: Applications across disorders and settings.* New York, NY: Guilford Press.

Koons, C. R., Robins, C. J., Tweed, J. L., Lynch, T. R., Gonzalez, A. M., Morse, J. Q., et al. (2001). Efficacy of dialectical behavior therapy in women veterans with borderline personality disorder. *Behavior Therapy, 32*(2), 371–390.

Linehan, M. M. (1993a). *Cognitive-behavioral treatment of borderline personality disorder.* New York, NY: Guilford Press.

Linehan, M. M. (1993b). *Skills training manual for treating borderline personality disorder.* New York, NY: Guilford Press.

Linehan, M. M. (1997). Validation and psychotherapy. In A. Bohart & L. Greenberg (Eds.), *Empathy reconsidered: New directions in psychotherapy* (pp. 353–392). Washington, D.C.: American Psychological Association.

Linehan, M. M., Armstrong, H. E., Suarez, A., Allmon, D., & Heard, H. L. (1991). Cognitive-behavioral treatment of chronically parasuicidal borderline patients. *Archives of General Psychiatry, 48*(12), 1060–1064.

Linehan, M. M., Comtois, K. A., Murray, A. M., Brown, M. Z., Gallop, R. J., Heard, H. L., et al. (2006). Two-year randomized controlled trial and follow-up of dialectical behavior therapy vs. therapy by experts for suicidal behaviors and borderline personality disorder. *Archives of General Psychiatry, 63*(7), 757–766.

Linehan, M. M., Dimeff, L. A., Reynolds, S. K., Comtois, K. A., Welch, S. S., Heagerty, P., et al. (2002). Dialectical behavior therapy versus comprehensive validation therapy plus 12-step for the treatment of opioid dependent women meeting criteria for borderline personality disorder. *Drug and Alcohol Dependence, 67*(1), 13–26.

Linehan, M. M., Schmidt, H., Dimeff, L. A., Craft, J. C., Kanter, J., & Comtois, K. A. (1999). Dialectical behavior therapy for patients with borderline personality disorder and drug-dependence. *American Journal on Addictions, 8*(4), 279–292.

McMain, S., Guimond, T., Streiner, D., Cardish, R. J., & Links, P. (2012). Clinical outcomes and functioning post-treatment: A two-year follow-up of dialectical behavior therapy versus general psychiatric management for borderline personality disorder. *American Journal of Psychiatry, 169*(6), 650–661.

McMain, S. F., Links, P. S., Gnam, W. H., Guimond, T., Cardish, R. J., Korman, L., et al. (2009). A randomized trial of dialectical behavior therapy versus general psychiatric management for borderline personality disorder. *American Journal of Psychiatry, 166*(12), 1365–1374.

Miller, A. L., Rathus, J. H., & Linehan, M. M. (2007). *Dialectical behavior therapy with suicidal adolescents.* New York, NY: Guilford Press.

Ravitz, P., Cooke, R.G., Mitchell, S., Reeves, S., Teshima, J., Lokuge, B., . . . Zaretsky, A. (2013). Continuing education to go: Capacity building in psychotherapies for front-line mental health workers in underserviced communities. *Canadian Journal of Psychiatry, 58* (6).

Soler, J., Pascual, J. C., Tiana, T., Cebria, A., Barrachina, J., Campins, M. J., et al. (2009). Dialectical behavior therapy skills training compared to standard group therapy in borderline personality disorder: A 3-month randomised controlled clinical trial. *Behavior Research and Therapy, 47*(5), 353–358.

Turner, R. M. (2000). Naturalistic evaluation of dialectical behavior therapy-oriented treatment for borderline personality disorder. *Cognitive and Behavioral Practice, 7*(4), 413–419.

Verheul, R., van den Bosch, L. M. C., Koeter, M. W. J., de Ridder, M. A. J., Stijnen, T., & van den Brink, W. (2003). Dialectical behavior therapy for women with borderline personality disorder: Twelve-month, randomised clinical trial in the Netherlands. *British Journal of Psychiatry, 182*, 135–140.